BUILDINGS THAT CREATE JOBS

For information, contact: www.mancusogroup.com

This book is available in paperback, hardcover, and eBook.

Cover design by 846 Global Publishing

Printed in the United States of America

ISBN: 979-8-9883264-0-3

In honor of my father,
Joseph L. Mancuso,
for showing us how to use
whatever we have to encourage
whatever is possible.

BUILDINGS THAT CREATE JOBS
by B. Thomas Mancuso

TABLE OF CONTENTS

INTRODUCTION

My father, Joseph L. Mancuso, became famous as the originator of the business incubation concept when he launched the Batavia Industrial Center [BIC]. I grew up playing and sweeping floors in that building. Later, I had the privilege of working with him for decades in this business model he founded to help other entrepreneurs and reenergize communities. We talked for years about writing down the things we learned from our many projects to help others that might attempt similar work. This is my effort at writing that book.

This is not an exhaustively researched, data-driven tome. Business incubation is not a textbook activity. The real learning is done on the ground — in the buildings and struggling communities. Besides, each project is an individual medley of resources and strategies, making it difficult to establish a standard operating procedure that works for all incubators. Starting in 1959, and ever since, we have confronted an endless variety of unique situations as we sought to nurture businesses wherever we were asked to help. Our goal to create jobs was always in focus as we worked to revive dilapidated buildings, improve people's lives, strengthen community economies, and, often, all of the above.

After creating and filling the world's first business incubator with companies and facilitating the creation of hundreds of jobs (learning a lot of things the hard way during that journey), the success of filling the industrial center [BIC] led to requests to fill empty factories in other places. Over more than 60 years since then, we have worked in many communities with a collection of properties that have included a 9,000-square-foot [SF]commercial building, a hospital, and a million-square-foot factory campus. The communities we've worked in span a spectrum from small (population 2,000) to typical (population 10,000 to 50,000) to metropolitan areas of more than a million. We've had the honor of helping thousands of businesses as they created several thousand jobs. We "learned by doing," but it took decades to accumulate our experience and develop a system.

We have always defined a *business incubator* as "a place that helps people start and grow businesses that create jobs in a community." Our specific intention is to serve startups and small businesses by providing an affordable work environment along with assistance for their sorts of needs. There are many buildings that serve small and micro businesses without a structured program that are not "intentional incubators" but, because they are operated with benevolent and nurturing management, may contribute to boosting their local economy and job creation. We call these sorts of projects a "Local Business Center" [LBC]. Much of what we prescribe for incubators can be applied to LBCs as well.

Given its economic development mission, it surprises people that the BIC was a for-profit enterprise. However, it never occurred to my uncles when they decided to buy that empty factory that they should not earn some money while helping to fix the local unemployment disaster.

We have owned and operated our own spaces, managed spaces on behalf of government-affiliated entities, and become deeply familiar with all models of incubation through participation in national and local trade associations. There is often an expectation that "mission-driven" projects can only be sincerely done by not-for-profit entities. Our experience proves that success in the "buildings for jobs" sector can be achieved from almost any platform as long as the project creates enough real value for everyone involved. **Many have said,**

2

"There is no mission without margin." I always give credit to hospital administrator Sister Margaret Mary Hughes for teaching me that in action. We cannot take care of those who need us if we are not healthy enough to do what they need us to do for as long as they need us to do it.

We have filled and sold LOTS of B.O.B.'s [Big Old Buildings]. Some fellow experienced industrial adaptive reuse practitioners call them by the more colorful "Big Uglies" moniker. Whatever you call them, they are both a challenge and an opportunity to make a positive difference in their home community through strategic revitalization.

This book's chapters are organized into the primary lessons we have learned:

1. Real Business incubators work.
2. Be jobs-focused & place-based.
3. Strive for inclusivity, diversity & mixed use.
4. Be locally owned & operated.
5. Find ways to help them.
6. Strive for financial independence.
7. Recycled buildings can save time and money.
8. Size Matters.
9. Plant a tree – Start now!

Every property "has its own unique personality," according to my friend and adaptive reuse innovator, Steve Asbury. Unlocking this puzzle with the purpose to "Fill the building, create jobs, and make money" has been our family mission since 1959. We employ innovation and creativity to unravel the mystery of how to recycle something like a 200,000 SF factory building to replace lost jobs or just not be an eyesore anymore. This is almost always a bootstrap adventure because normally there is little or no money. Strategies that worked for us regarding leasing, facility operations, funding, etc. may help you breathe new life into an old building you are saving or a business incubator you are starting or expanding.

The need for hometown, community-centric, job-focused, locally sustainable business nurturing places has in no way diminished. Whatever you call it — incubator, accelerator, innovation hub, or just "business-friendly place" — startups, local independent businesses, communities, and empty buildings need them. So many times in distressed communities, the answer is right there in some empty, obsolete building IF it can be revived in a practical, local-market, respectful manner. We desire to encourage and share our practical experiences with those around the world who might strive to take responsibility for the success and prosperity of their community into their own hands.

The fact this has been done, many times, can give you the confidence to start and, when needed, provide a beacon of hope that you can do it. With stories and examples, and shared concepts from thousands of successful deals and projects (plus some that failed), you may find a process, procedure, or principle that you've been looking for to get you through some challenges that may have been blocking your progress.

Expect stories and observations from more than 60 years of effort filling existing buildings with businesses to create prosperity for all involved. The small business owner incubatees, their employees, the project developers, and the local tax base are just a few examples of the beneficiaries of such an endeavor. We have learned by doing. The lessons we share are the result of many solutions we devised and many mistakes along the way — mistakes you don't have to make.

If you're thinking about starting a business incubator, this book will help you decipher between actually starting an incubator, a real estate project, or something else altogether. In any event, you will find some tips to help you on your way. Together, we will explore:

- What buildings/projects might work
- How you will deliver a value-creating program for your market
- Where the money will come from.

If you already have an incubator project started, you will learn:

- How to increase revenue through leasing & pricing
- How to attract new businesses
- Ideas to reduce costs while maintaining quality management.

I hope that somewhere in the following pages you will learn something about planning, starting, and operating a successful business incubator or local business center in your town and that you will find a "nugget or two" of practical wisdom.

My father and I have made two lifetimes' worth of good and bad decisions while working to create jobs and prosperity for people by recycling old factories in their community. Our perspective, gained through over six decades of organizing, revitalizing, and operating job-creating buildings, is uniquely grounded in practical reality. We hope that you can learn something from our hard-won experience that will help your project succeed sooner and more abundantly.

We wish you much success as you move forward!

Chapter 1 — Real Business Incubators Work

BIC was the first business incubator in the world. However, the activity existed before the name. And it all started with one industrious family. The organized activity of attracting, creating, and assisting businesses to produce local jobs was born in 1959 as a private-sector solution to an economic development disaster in a small community.

The Mancuso Family originally emigrated from Vallelunga, Sicily to the sugar and cotton fields near New Orleans, Louisiana in America. They were lured from the Big Easy to a spot just 6 hours west of the Big Apple — Batavia, New York, by the growing number of available construction laborer jobs to build an expansion of the city's largest industrial employer, the Johnston Harvester Works, in 1907. From construction, they moved to factory jobs in the new malleable foundry they helped build. Respiratory problems led my grandfather, Rosalino "Benjamin" Mancuso, to leave the factory, attend a trade school, and become a licensed plumber. From this foundation, the family added a plumbing & hardware store, restaurant, bowling alley, movie theater, and multiple auto dealerships over the next few decades.

By the time Massey-Harris Limited (successor to Johnston Harvester Works) closed its factory in 1958 the Mancuso enterprises were significant and deeply intertwined into the fabric of their adopted hometown. Faced with more than 20% unemployment in their immediate market, these immigrant family businesspeople took it upon themselves to try to save their new community by replacing the gaping economic hole created by the closing of the Massey-Harris factory, Batavia's largest employer. The family gambled that they could find a single large employer to occupy the sprawling 1 million SF industrial campus (parts of which, built in 1882, were already 70 years old at that time) and replace the lost jobs. Joe Mancuso, a World War II veteran and manager of the hardware store, was put in charge of the campus and given this job: *"Fill the building, create jobs, and make money."* This has been The Mancuso Group's mission ever since.

When it became obvious that securing a large replacement employer could not be found, they pivoted to a new strategy. In the words of my father, Joe Mancuso **"We will do whatever is needed to attract people to start, locate, and grow their businesses in Batavia."** That philosophy and strategy are the foundation of what we now know as business incubators.

Joe and his team set their sights on a new mission: instead of trying to market the total 1 million SF of the factory as a single parcel to one company, spaces of all sizes, flexible leases, shared staff, shared equipment, and all sorts of incentives and assistance were imagined and implemented to bring job-creating businesses to the facility.

There may be no better example of what was to come than the Batavia Industrial Center's very first business, Batavia Sign. It would start with only two jobs and 1,200 SF (something was better than nothing). Batavia Sign's financial resources were so limited, the BIC helped fund their startup by ordering a package of signage that included the iconic two-story metal sign that still hangs over the main entrance at 56 Harvester Avenue.

When Joe Mancuso attracted this first business, helping to fund them by purchasing — and prepaying — for a 20' metal sign, renting them a small flexible space, and creating a path for them to launch, it started a practice of imaginative "bootstrapping" in the interest of local job creation that continues today. This implementation of innovative, practical, value-producing, win-win solutions to the myriad challenges of startup and enterprise lifecycle faced by small and growing businesses, often delivered from scarce resources, is a hallmark of a business incubator.

As a witness to his first project's success, Joe Mancuso's ability to successfully fill that old factory with businesses that generated hundreds of jobs led to requests to perform similar "magic" for other distressed places and vacant properties. Efforts to fill a million-square-foot vacant industrial factory and replace thousands of lost jobs began with this "drop in the ocean" that would eventually start a flood. Today, various estimates count 9,000 to 14,000 business incubators around the world.

The privilege of helping to improve many diverse challenging situations continually teaches us about a number of things that work, as well as a bunch that do not. But the goal was the same, "Fill the building, create jobs, and make money." Joe Mancuso was walking a NY Times reporter through an 80-year-old industrial attic full of chickens from a nearby commercial hatchery that was one of the many new job-producing activities at the bustling Batavia Industrial Center in the early 1960s. In his matter-of-fact manner, he was explaining how his efforts had transformed a vacant million-square-foot factory in Upstate NY into a thriving collection of small, medium, and growing businesses that now employed hundreds of local people. Responding to the reporter's question, Joe quipped, "They're incubating chickens, and I'm incubating businesses."

A business incubator, as defined by the guy that invented it, is **a place that helps people start and grow businesses that create jobs in your community**. You can differentiate one from its fraternal twin, the Local Business Center because the incubator will have a more robust program of support services, resource sharing, and networking activities. Both are vital economic development tools that are situationally appropriate. However, if there's no program or culture of enterprise encouragement, you probably just have a real estate project, which can still be a "coincidental" job generator.

From our experience, a business incubator has three main characteristics:

- **It's a place** - a physical building or portion of a building that gets filled with businesses.
- **It assists people to startup and grow businesses** - using small, flexible spaces, affordable rents, training, networking, and other appropriate support.
- **It produces jobs** - by attracting businesses that hire people and generate local prosperity.

It should be said here, to be very clear, that when this book, and we, at the Mancuso Business Development Group, talk about business incubators, we primarily mean a **job-focused, community-centric project**. These are, most often, developed and operated by economic development-focused local organizations, transitioning businesses, or strategic real estate investors. You will hear and read about various sorts of things called incubators, accelerators, innovation centers, and other exciting names that measure their success in capital raised or technology advanced or grants and patents secured. We recognize there is value in all of these things but, for us, incubators are unique in that they are primarily focused on boosting prosperity in their home community. It has been that way since the beginning.

Stabilized, mature business incubator projects feature jobs at startups in the facility, jobs in the community at businesses that have graduated from the center, and a recognized and active role as a dynamic component of the region's economic progress and entrepreneurial ecosystem. In Batavia, NY, and other municipalities that are home to a business incubator in a recycled factory building, there are properties that have been assessed for millions of dollars, occupied by incubator graduates (businesses that have grown enough to "leave the nest" to lease, buy or build space for their prospering enterprise), paying property taxes that benefit the entire hometown. Furthermore, many jobs are added to the community and an obsolete building is rescued from blight.

The center is often "fuel" for the economic engine but, sometimes, it IS the engine!

Across millions of square feet leased and thousands of jobs that have been created from our work, a sample of "what an incubator does" to fill a building with businesses and jobs includes:

- **Startup-sized space increments** – Units could be as small as 100 SF for an office, 600 SF for an industrial space, or whatever suits the market.
- **Flexible sizes** – The larger size of the building allows companies to flex up and down, reducing the risk of "wrong size" leasing while figuring out the "right size" or scaling up as it grows.
- **Affordable** - "Back door finance" reduces operating costs by sharing resources that may include space, assets, and people. This maximizes the impact of startup funds for businesses because they "don't need to fund what they don't need to pay."
- **Flexible rent** - Graduated rent schedules tied to a business plan are common tools to lower occupancy costs.
- **Speed** - Need to "strike while the iron's hot?" We always tried to have a few "same day" spaces for tenants needing immediate space solutions.
- **Easy** – Utilities provided by the incubator save time, money, and cash in monthly fees, utility deposits, and disconnection charges upon moving for the fledgling enterprises.
- **Information** - Many startups are "below the radar" to government, EDO, financial, educational, and other institutions that want to help them. The ability to open and facilitate "lines of communication" within the ecosystem is a valuable business incubator role.

- **Networking connections** – In addition to the above connections, close proximity to other entrepreneurs and/or access to business mentors and community support helps to ease the "lonely entrepreneur" syndrome for some solos and encourages "creative collisions" for everyone's benefit.
- **Shared assets (physical and human)** - We've shared semi-trucks, forklifts, operating and clerical labor, and more in efforts to stretch precious cash while maximizing productivity for survival and progress.

Reducing the entrepreneur's risk is the common denominator. Starting and operating your own business is not for the fainthearted with 20 percent of startups failing in the first year and 70 percent crashing in the next two to five years. A business incubator can't eliminate all of the dangers, but when it fills the right gaps and delivers appropriate support, the survival rate improves. This, then, leads to jobs in the incubator, many of which eventually spill outside and into the host community. The Batavia-style solution, originally executed by a private effort, for many years, was a common response to a significant job loss if there was any response at all. Local initiatives led by hometown businesspeople, chambers of commerce, or ad hoc community groups either took some sort of action in their own economic salvation or nothing happened at all as the community continued its downward slide.

Over the years more incubators appeared. It has become an industry that continues to evolve. A brief recap of the Stages of Business Incubation Evolution* looks like this:

First Generation. (*late 1950s – mid 1980s*) Initiation and development of the concept. We call this the "Infrastructure: economies of scale" period.
- BIs provided low-cost space and a small set of shared services.
- Business Incubators were considered a new economic development tool.

Second Generation. (*mid 1980s – mid 1990s*). Active growth and development. "Business support: accelerating the learning curve" is the name of this period.

- The industry added coaching and training support, including knowledge-based services, to accelerate the learning curve.
- Governments in Europe and the U. S. realized that innovation and entrepreneurship were cornerstones of economic development.
- Universities and research centers tap their resources for the transfer of knowledge and commercialization of products and services.

Third Generation. (*mid 1990s – present*). Industry maturity and new leaps of development. "Networks & Value Chains" are this period's common characteristics.

- Access to technological, professional, and financial networks enhanced the startup process.
- The search for fast access to capital and new knowledge became one of the most important tasks for entrepreneurs.
- We saw the rise of for-profit internet incubators.

*(synthesized from works of Bruneel, Ratinho, Clarysse, Groen, (2012) and Lalkaka (2000) by Vasily Ryzhonkov)

As the industry sectors have evolved and stratified, it seems that the local job creation focus often gets overlooked in the relentless race for venture capital and technology innovation. It has narrowed opportunities for all others as financiers search for the next "gazelles" and "unicorns" that can scale fast and wide nationally or globally. Accelerators, innovation centers or zones, specialty incubators, and other such entrepreneurial-aimed efforts all have their place. We respect the value of every sincere business development endeavor.

David Hochman says it well in this quote from his *Business Incubation in New York State* chapter in Sarfraz Mian's book of collected research on incubators and accelerators:

> *"To emphasize: some startups that will never attract VC investment because the 'economics' do not work for VC investment partnerships can still be taxpayers, employers, wealth-creators, innovators, and sources of second-generation spinoffs that rapidly accelerate a regional economy. Incubators, far more than seed-venture accelerators are learning this lesson and targeting these companies, even when VC investors spurn them."*

From the concept's genesis, improving the economic situation of people in a place has been an inextricable component of the motivation. This is why, in our view, a **business incubator always means community job focus.**

So how do you recognize a business incubator? First, it's a place, a physical place, a building, or a collection of buildings. Second, it is, or is striving hard to be, full of businesses. The third and defining characteristic is that it actively welcomes small and startup enterprises and works to help them survive, grow, and prosper while producing jobs for local people. As the years pass, some of those incubatees will strengthen enough to move out into the community by leasing, buying, or building a space, thus making room for the next fledgling business to move in and, hopefully, repeat the cycle. All of this grew out of Joe Mancuso's efforts.

The physical places we have chosen in our work have always been existing surplus factories, commercial buildings, or institutional buildings. They have come to us for any number of reasons, including:

- The former business closed and left town.
- The former business is downsizing and struggling to carry (or seeks to maximize the value of) surplus space.
- The building is too big for the market.

14

- The building is obsolete for its original use.
- The building or campus is "complicated."

Generally speaking, we prefer existing buildings for reasons that include reviving their historic place as significant employers in the community and contributing to environmental and financial sustainability by avoiding blight and demolition. Sometimes it's a blessing to work with an existing space and, many times, it is a challenge to discern the revitalization path that best realizes the objectives of the project developer or operator. While, as you might imagine, nonprofit and for-profit developers/operators have differences in "why" they tackle one of these, their efforts to fill them will drive some complementary practices.

When working to make the best use of time, money, and situational realities in a job-focused community endeavor, some common characteristics include:

- Multi-tenant approach - Fill a BIG space with a greater number of smaller uses.
- Market-driven, mixed-use approach- Better reflects the fabric of the community, better captures local opportunity, and encourages the diversity that tends to improve the campus community and creativity while also reducing risk by spreading it over a broader base.
- Better asset sharing - such as larger commercial infrastructure than is normally available to small/micro biz (truck docks, sprinklers, HVAC, etc.).

Hometown jobs for our neighbors and our people are always, to us, what a business incubator is about. Business incubators come in all shapes and sizes to serve communities of all shapes and sizes. We believe, and our experience confirms for us, that these are important activities for a community or owner of a certain sort of building. Properly structured and managed, they can be financially sustainable and independent, as we will address in further detail in future chapters.

15

Incubators are incubators because they find a way that works to encourage the creation of jobs in that place. If flexible spaces and rents are needed, they are provided. If community networking is needed, it's developed. Should shared services become a need, the incubator finds a way to provide them. Incubators are focused on the survival and success of their occupants because that's where the jobs come from.

LESSON #1 IS THAT REAL BUSINESS INCUBATORS WORK

CHAPTER 1 REVIEW

- A job-focused business incubator looks for buildings because businesses that need people need space for their team to operate. Because of the integral contribution of physical space to this process, there is an attractive symmetry in combining the efforts to revive a blighted empty factory or commercial property with the nurturing and encouraging efforts to help a new enterprise startup and grow to create and spread local prosperity.

- BIs are places with a variety of types and sizes of space with flexible affordable rental options and services that meet the needs of its clients or tenants.

- The mission is to *"Fill the building, create jobs, and make money."*

- The BI is a place (physical place), it assists entrepreneurs, and it produces jobs.

- BIs are community-centered and community-focused.

Chapter 2 — Be Jobs-Focused & Place-Based

"Fill the building, create jobs, and make money."

The question is often asked, "Why an incubator" and/or "Why YOUR incubator?" My answer is formed by various combinations of the objectives delivered to my father, Joe Mancuso, by his father, Benjamin (Rosalino) Mancuso, as his "marching orders" to conquer the challenge of Batavia's economic mess.

The Market Mismatch™

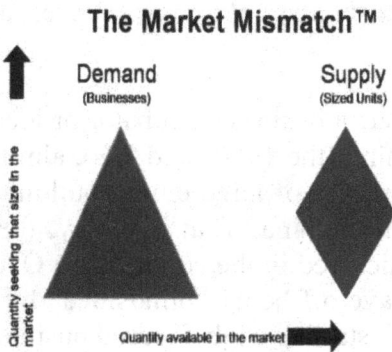

Demand (Businesses)   Supply (Sized Units)

Quantity seeking that size in the market

Quantity available in the market

The Market Mismatch™ is an integral component concept of The Strategic Building Solution™

Mission-driven incubators often target blighted buildings for entrepreneurial encouragement and job creation. **Margin driven** projects may see a "bargain" purchase with an opportunity to take advantage of the inherent "Market Mismatch" that exists in many markets, relating to small industrial, commercial, and office space.

Depending on your initiating perspective, you may "lean" more toward a **mission-driven** endeavor or a more **margin-driven** local business center. Both of these pathways encourage small businesses and create jobs. To design and build a productive, resilient, business incubator program, it is vital to be clear about the measurable results desired from your business development project. Making jobs the primary focus doesn't make the project easier, but it does help clarify the myriad of decisions you'll be making along the way.

To be clear, the first focus is to attract and grow jobs, and the second, and inseparable focus, is that those jobs can be appropriate and enduring for your location. Active community leadership, investment, and participation are significant keys to devising an effective program and process for your place.

We typically think of this primary market as that area within the circle of what we call **Entrepreneurial Gravity™**. It's been our experience that 80% of the business owners that gravitate to your center will live within a 15 to 20-minute commute of the facility. That constitutes your primary market. This is a reality that challenges smaller markets. While rural startups may be willing to travel a little longer, you're still confronted with smaller populations. You have to figure out how to make your facility work at the level that's appropriate for the size and the activity level of your market. As President Theodore Roosevelt would say, **"Do what you can, with what you've got, where you are."**

There are a variety of reasons to pursue a business incubator or local business center project. In the beginning (the 1960s and 70s), almost all incubator projects were adaptive reuses of large empty buildings inspired by significant local economic trauma. That is to say, they were reactive, sparked by an economic need in the community. Over time, proactive efforts emerged to stave off being "blindsided" by a disaster. Some examples of reasons for starting a job-focused business center we've seen include the following:

- Replace lost jobs   [MISSION thru margin]
- Create new jobs   [MISSION thru margin]
- Initiate more economic diversity and prosperity
  [MISSION thru margin]
- Fill a larger-than-market industrial, commercial, or
  institutional building [MARGIN thru mission]
- Revitalize an obsolete or underutilized property
  [MARGIN thru mission]
- Enlightened self-interest [better businesses make better
  tenants which results in better-performing properties]
  [MARGIN thru mission]

Either effort can serve the needs of small and micro business enterprises by encouraging business and generating job growth. Offering manageably sized affordable spaces in the 100 SF to 3,000 SF range delivers approachable startup locations that might not exist otherwise. If the host facility is of sufficient size, it can also service mid-size firms (10,000 to 30,000 SF manufacturing) and second-step graduating incubatees.

It should be noted that even a reputedly for-profit real estate investment property that serves industrial, commercial, and/or office tenants can respond to its own "enlightened self-interest" by finding ways to help its "arms-length" commercial clients operate better businesses. In doing so, the commercial landlord will benefit from more successful tenants that, in turn, pay rent on time, support more jobs, and potentially lease more space.

Government and universities increased their involvement in the 1980s, and a majority of American business incubators came to be developed by educational institutions. A focus grew on maximizing their innovation and research to capture higher potential opportunities for scalable, higher-value concepts. We have all witnessed the explosive growth of the "gazelles" (fast-growing companies whose revenues increase substantially within the first five years) and "unicorns" (startups that demand estimated or stock values of a billion dollars or more) that path has delivered. The jobs, quality of life, and financial positives are undeniable.

Every community does not have a university or a pool of venture capital. What every settled place <u>does</u> have are people and a need for everyone's financial security and well-being. Because most communities are a heterogeneous assortment of people and abilities, the spectrum of business opportunities that are encouraged and supported wants to be as broad as possible. For this reason, our experience has taught us that *"Every business is important because every job is important."*

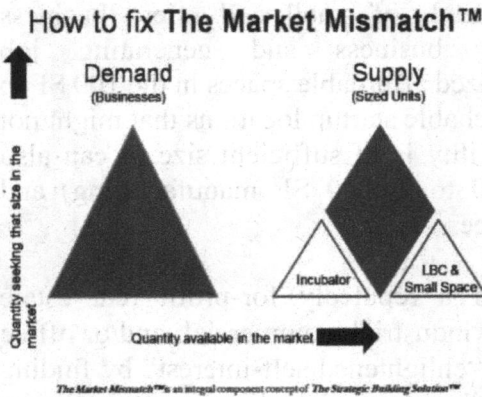

How to fix **The Market Mismatch**™

One of the keys to success in community job creation is to tell the truth, and to go to the sectors where those jobs are most likely to be. The starting point for actual community economic progress is micro and small enterprises. I refer here to true "small," not the SBA 500 jobs' definition of "small." According to the 2020 U. S. Census, business establishments with less than five full-time employees comprise over 55% of the eight million U. S. businesses (for Canada and Europe this percentage is even higher). When you add to this base those firms employing nineteen or fewer, the share grows to 73%. Despite this reality, in most markets, the supply of industrial and commercial space for smaller businesses is generally far below the demand. Cowork operations, where they exist, slightly ease this mismatch for office users. A business incubator that services micro and small industrial/commercial clients can be an immediate benefit to this sector and its corresponding job opportunities.

22

It is important to everyone's success, survival, and satisfaction that the incubator effort serves the core local entrepreneurial DNA while also respectfully welcoming and, over time, weaving in the unexpected variety of other businesses that invariably will show up. Some places have a heritage of metal trades or food processing or something else. These historic foundations can be a valuable place to start shaping your building and program. Beyond this, there can be some unique mix already in place of other makers, services, and activities that can benefit from a nurturing environment. As people and economies evolve, stuff no one ever thought of will arise and create new opportunities for innovation.

Just as "every building has a unique personality that needs to be discovered and respected" according to successful rehab expert, Steve Asbury, I have experienced that each community is imbued with a distinct, unrepeatable identity that needs to be honored. It is exactly the complication of the infinite variety of these sorts of combinations that make it so important to respect and address local realities in each project. Given the seriousness of both disciplines, it is wise to include some experienced professionals with local leadership and participation in creating **The Strategic Blueprint™** for your project. In addition to saving time and money, an objective perspective is critical in deciding if there are enough local resources to produce a viable business incubator.

Many large buildings struggle to stay productive and relevant after they've outlived their original use. The adaptive reuse of recycling these obsolete "Big Uglies" into dynamic hives of entrepreneurial activity can be positive for everyone involved in that community:

- The building gets reused.
- Business owners have a supportive "right-sized" place to locate.
- Local people get jobs.
- Property Owner/Project Sponsor makes money.

We have found that, in many ways, large, old industrial, commercial, and institutional buildings offer built-in advantages to being recycled for small businesses. To start, they tend to be located in pedestrian and vehicle-accessible locations. Their historic inflow of people and other resources make them recognizable as places that contribute to the community's quality of life. With some older factories, there can be strong, multi-generational connections for people to that place that enhance its community value. From an infrastructure perspective, larger facilities often feature more robust utility services and loading area options that, otherwise, would not be accessible to growing businesses and startups. In the same vein, fire protection systems, cafeteria kitchens, and elevators are examples of other leftover assets available in these sorts of properties that a small enterprise might not be able to access otherwise.

Just the fact that the building structure exists can contribute to progress. It can be cost-prohibitive to build a little building. The ability to occupy some part of a property that's already there reduces time and cost for the startup. It is not uncommon for "leftover buildings" to already reflect local needs for HVAC or geographical legacy businesses in a way that may activate or accelerate threads of local business DNA. Therein, we find another instance of the special sort of synergy that can energize a job and business development project that truly is connected with and reflects the reality of its place.

At its heart, an incubator is people helping people create opportunities for people in their hometown. The incubator operators help business owners start and grow businesses that employ people who frequent other businesses, pay taxes, and continue a spiral of prosperity for everyone it touches. It is for this reason that we are committed to, and have been so dedicated to, a continuation and improvement of this process wherever possible.

In the Mancuso Business Development world, a business nurturing facility doesn't need to be recognized or certified by anyone as an "official incubator" in order to actually perform the incubation service. In order to access certain grants or support funding, however, it may help to have some official recognition and non-profit structure. Still, doing the work and getting the results have always seemed a better indicator to me. There is much talk today about innovation centers, venture capital accelerators, and tech-specific incubators of all shapes and sizes. While there's certainly room in the world for all sorts of business development incubator programs, for us it's always been about jobs — local jobs. Ideally, they become "sticky" jobs that will start and stay in the home community and bring prosperity for years.

"Every business is in some stage of leaving your town."

This hard-won bit of wisdom was first shared by my Dad in the 1960s and is a core reason that economic development, including a job-creating business incubator, is a forever job. In our ever-changing world, technology shifts, businesses get sold, some fail, business owners retire, get sick or die, and myriad other events terminate local enterprises. It may happen in 50 years, but it could also be tomorrow. It's not just the old businesses that are vulnerable to move or collapse, even that shiny new startup will be gone someday. We have seen two global corporations partner on a $380 million joint venture that was promised to provide "hundreds of jobs" and then totally abandon the unrealized results within only three years. Many economic development organizations (EDO) lack the staff or funding to do all of the things needed in their territory. Scarce time and resources often force them to focus on only the bigger project opportunities, which leaves small and micro enterprises unsupported. Well-run business incubators or local business centers can be very cost-effective tools for a community or economic development group to protect and nurture this vital component of the local prosperity ecosystem.

Business incubator startups are only one part of the story. As they grow and advance through stages of the business lifecycle, many

25

"graduate" from the incubator and lease, buy, or build "next-step" local facilities. At one time, every old industrial building in Batavia was occupied by a graduate of the Batavia Industrial Center. An example of this is seen in a 17,000 SF factory on Franklin Street that has been "home" to three successive BIC graduates! The ongoing operation of a locally consistent business startup and development center embeds itself into the fabric of the regional entrepreneurial ecosystem. It is positive when a market develops second-step space with buildings to buy and, when needed, land for new construction. Most enterprises are small before they're ever big, and many happily operate in the middle, but a hometown business incubator can serve them all.

Incubation, like all economic development, is not "one and done." Opportunities are always coming and going, while the world is constantly changing. Day by day and year by year, what is needed to succeed will evolve. Your best chance to get the outcomes your place wants is to "take the reins" and tailor an ongoing program that reflects the way you want it to function. Locally owned businesses tend to be more long-term.

As companies mature, many will leave the incubator and move to larger facilities within the **Entrepreneurial Gravity™** field of the business development center, helping to further the overall goal of building local enterprise. This is another reason why organizing a diverse, mixed-use, job-focused incubator that matches the unique character of your community can be "the gift that keeps giving." In our experience, a self-sustaining business incubator can be the foundation and one of the funding sources for such an independent community effort.

People and communities come in all shapes and sizes. It is <u>so</u> important for initial and ongoing local input to help capture true hometown DNA instead of trying to "shoehorn" a mismatch by attempting to force a fintech or medtech (or any-specific-tech-of-the-month) focus into a place that has historically been more rural/agricultural or "other tech" oriented. True, it is wise to "take all comers," including whatever tech actually shows up, and either have in-house or partnership resources for the exotic stuff, but a solid local response to your common core enterprise and artisan clients is the best recipe for long-term impact on the local community.

Another ingredient that comes "in all shapes, sizes, and sorts" is the building that houses a successful business incubator program. While we'll come back to this in future chapters, it is important to remember that the building and its operation is key to the job creation, financial success, and sustainability of the BI. The ability to "make money" for the sponsor or property owner is a critical attraction, and a challenge, to the startup and survival of a BI and/or LBC. While grants and subsidies are useful in the early years, they are seldom secure for decades. Strategizing, planning, and operating the building in a profitable MISSION/MARGIN balance, consistent with your vision is the key to the financial independence needed to remain effective in responding to your community's/market's needs over the years. To us, it is all inextricably interwoven:

The program attracts and assists the businesses
that fill the building and create jobs so that the
project sponsor can make the money to be
financially strong and independent enough to
relentlessly improve the program and building to
keep the cycle going.

We believe that what makes an incubator successful is a local sponsor with a realistic financial and operating plan, a long-term strategy, and a commitment that is led by active, dedicated, caring local leaders, investors, and supporters. It is a place and a program focused on the unique DNA and realities of that community. Nobody cares more about your community and understands its culture and history than the people who live in it.

Wherever you start and whatever your goal —creating jobs or filling a building or making money— a business incubator or Local Business Center can be the solution that promotes progress and prosperity for people in your hometown for years to come.

LESSON #2 IS THAT INCUBATORS SHOULD BE JOB-FOCUSED AND PLACE-BASED

CHAPTER 2 REVIEW

- Your BI may either "lean" more toward a **mission-driven** or a more margin-driven endeavor.

- Community leadership, investment, and participation are critical to a program's success.

- **Entrepreneurial Gravity™** is a phenomenon that leads 80% of the business owners that utilize your center to live within a 15 to 20-minute commute of the facility.

- BIs often replace lost jobs, create new jobs, and revitalize obsolete or underutilized property, among many other Margin- or mission-based motivators.

- Governments and universities often drive the development of BIs.

- Successful BIs tend to respect the local entrepreneurial DNA.

- BIs come in all shapes, sizes, and sorts just like buildings that house them.

Chapter 3 — Strive For Inclusivity, Diversity, & Mixed-Use

"Ever since the beginning to keep the world spinning, it takes all kinds of kinds."

—All Kinds of Kinds by Miranda Lambert

Our communities, and the entire world, are heterogeneous collections of lives and processes. We strongly believe that helping folks learn to profitably navigate that reality is an important part of teaching them to build successful enterprises.

To accomplish the feat of building a strong business incubator, diversity (many kinds of diversity) must be sought. Diversity is a gift that keeps on giving to everyone involved because innovation is accelerated in a mixed-use environment. This is particularly true at a job-focused business incubator that is striving to maximize the business and employment potential in a community.

Mixed-use means a blend of industrial, commercial, office, and other business activities. The combinations and percentages will vary according to what is appropriate for the unique personality of your community. Your priorities and the realities of your facility and

31

situation will also affect the blend. In an old factory, there may be room for "everything." Conversely, in a repurposed department store or church, the structure may narrow the range of different activities that can be properly operated. The history of the community and the people still living there may impact the formula as well. The object here is to embrace a range of activities because it will benefit the incubatee, co-tenants, incubator, and home market at large.

Diversity is the variety within and across the mix of uses. While the humans behind the business may span any number of ages, education, sexual orientation, experience, ethnic groups, or financial capacity, the businesses themselves will do well to include whatever blend of startups, anchors, small corporates, and more stabilized enterprises as their situation calls for.

Everybody can benefit from diversity and inclusivity. Business incubators, properly run, create communities of opportunity, especially in their kaleidoscopic collection of clients. Diversity in mixed-use should be actively pursued. As we previously learned, *"Every business is important because every job is important."* The entrepreneurial incubatees can be exposed to a plethora of ideas and business models. Different ages, different uses and the intermingling of businesses in the building give each business a decided advantage. Furthermore, networking events encourage and increase the frequency of creative collisions that can inform and inspire more positive progress.

A medium to large-sized mixed-use, job-focused incubator has the additional advantage of being able to welcome businesses at various stages of the business life cycle, from startup to the growth and expansion phases to maturity and to exit. It's helpful for startup operators to see that some companies are exiting, so they might factor that into their company-building adventure. At the same time, folks in growth and mature business stages can see and be re-energized by the vitality and innovation of the startups. The opportunities for a diverse collection of companies to share and partner and provide value to each other that happen in an incubator are unlike anywhere else. At the incubator, they're encouraged to work together, they're actively connected by the building, they often patronize each other's businesses, and there's support for their individual needs. This sort of opportunity to uniquely add value through curated relationships is one of the great powers of incubator program networking. It's one of the reasons networking is such an important part of the program of almost every business incubator.

The incubator and its program also benefit in several ways. Housing multiple and diverse tenants spread the financial risk over a broader base of business sectors, enterprise life cycle stages, financial strengths, and seasonal variations. This means, for example, that while some people can pay market rent, others may be at only 25% of market rent and struggling to stay current.

Like any community or organism, every "piece of the puzzle" is in some different stage of its startup, growth, decline, or exit. Often, many of them can benefit from the wisdom, experience, or stories of their neighbors who have been through a similar situation. Another way the incubator benefits is that the very diversity of the tenant base adds value to the strength of the program by providing multiple perspectives. Diverse tenants, connected via the center's networking efforts, can help each other innovate by virtue of their various activities. We have seen a retailer's e-commerce activity inspire a center's job shop machinist to do more online sales, which then led to him doing additive manufacturing. In a physical sense, including various tenants of different sizes helps fill the nooks and crannies of any building, reducing unused space. This increased occupancy results in higher revenue which is the key to positive cash flow and the financial sustainability that we all crave.

On the other hand, there can be situationally strategic reasons to initiate a narrow sector or single tech incubator. Such a decision is not the shortest path to more local jobs and, almost always, results in the need to subsidize that effort throughout its lifetime. Given the history and reality of donor fatigue, this will shorten the life of the narrow or single-sector business incubator. We recognize that such programs need to exist, but we do not encourage such a path when jobs are your primary goal.

In addition to the programmatic value, there are business reasons why an incubator facility likes different-sized clients and tenants. Aside from the aforementioned risk-spreading benefits of entrepreneurs and businesses that are of different ages, a variety of business ownership structures, and diverse sectors, a spectrum of sizes helps fill the physical space and generate the revenue needed to cover operating and program costs. Having many tenants of different sizes and sectors reduces the risk of an "800 lb. gorilla" (large tenant) failing and endangering the health of the entire program. The project needs to be financially independent so that it can endure to serve the entrepreneurial needs of the ecosystem over the long term.

Another potential objective that medium to large space and programs can accommodate is the benefit derived from weaving some small corporates and/or an anchor tenant into the occupancy blend, from a financial strength and stability point of view. When a few corporate clients can be mixed in with independent local businesses, the corporates can be a good example of structure and branding that the startups may aspire to. We have found that, often, the corporate tenants in a job-focused business incubator are quick to participate in networking events, provide mentoring to the other clients, or share resources. In the meantime, project funders and lenders tend to take some comfort in the financial stability of these more established firms.

On a related note, anchor tenants can provide similar advantages. When facility space allows it, either during startup or at stabilization, sometimes a large or very established business can be a "gap filler" and provide financial support until the program stabilizes. In the beginning, this might last a year to three years, with the anchor eventually being "squeezed out" by incubatees. In a larger property, it will usually take longer before the anchor is replaced by smaller establishments. In either case, the program benefits are similar to small corporates, with the differentiator that anchors are more likely to be headquartered locally or regionally. These sorts of differences can improve the funding, networking, and operational strength that the incubator needs to provide an affordable, nurturing business environment for startups and small local businesses over the long term. The financial sustainability provided by this sort of diversity also contributes to progress for everyone it touches.

We started our business incubator lifetime by favoring industrial or manufacturing operations in job-focused business incubators because of their proven success as primary wealth generators. For us, our first dose of diversity came from opening up to office users. As economies evolved and manufacturing shrank as a share of the American (and global) economy, food, hospitality, personal services, technology, commercial activities, and whatever other uses were appropriate in that market came to be incorporated into these incubators and local business centers. This is an example of tailoring the project to the place that it serves.

In one small city, we manage a 500,000 SF building where the community has a propensity for manufacturing and making. The occupancy of that center skews heavily toward makers, machine shops, artisans, and independent manufacturers. One hundred miles away we manage another large building in another small city, but this one has an agricultural and food history. This job-focused, mixed-use incubator attracted a distillery and a state-funded, shared commercial kitchen. In both cases, the facility first develops the policies, procedures, and infrastructure that serve as primary job-creating activity (whatever that may be — manufacturing, software, food, etc.) and, then pursues and works to attract those businesses.

In every community we have ever served, the building could not be filled with a single homogeneous activity population. Although the building size can be a factor when it's medium to large (50,000 to 100,000 square feet and more), it is much more a reflection of the reality of any given regional economy. With that said, even if you could fill it with the same uses, you wouldn't want to.

There is another strategic advantage to different kinds of businesses because each sector has a different economic cycle rhythm and they're not all likely to fail or falter at the same time. If all of your clients serve the auto industry, in the event of an automotive downturn, the incubator is going to be in trouble as well as all of its clients and host community. We believe the best incubators resemble their community's strengths and unique DNA in their collection of industrial, commercial, office, and service business establishments. When housed together at a business incubator that provides assistance, training, and a nurturing environment, the community mix of businesses strengthens the incubator by blending the risk across sectors, business life cycles, and the spectrum of financial resources that support their ability to pay rent and other operating costs.

In a job-focused, mixed-use business incubator, most of your tenants will be independent local business owners that will look a lot like this (as described by author David S. Rose):

- They will likely be a solo founder.
- They will operate from a physical location (rather than a virtual home base).
- They will have fewer than ten employees.
- Their employees will not have equity.
- They will seek bank loans for financing.
- They quickly begin generating revenue.
- Their growth slows after profitability.
- 70% will have revenues under $1 million.
- Their jobs support their families.
- They will likely never seek nor have an exit[1]

---

[1]From The **Startup Checklist**: 25 Steps to a Scalable High-Growth Business by David S. Rose

Mix is a pivotal strategic decision that requires constant awareness. You can improve your chances to grow the appropriate entrepreneurial community for your mission and market by having an initial starting plan that considers how to attract your "targets" given the following:

- JOB DENSITY (jobs per square foot) – Job density varies by activity. Historically, it has been highest for offices at 1 per 200 SF and commercial uses closer to 1 per 500 SF. Industrial activities use the most space per job at 1 per 900 SF (*NB- calculations based on our experience).
- RENTAL RATES - Coincidentally, generally price per SF for space follows density, with office rates the highest per SF, followed by commercial, and industrial.
- STARTING SPACE NEEDS - What sorts of suite sizes and types will your property affordably accommodate?
- LOCAL MARKET DNA - Since you can't "push a rope uphill", what is the likely range of prospects and how does it relate to your mission and property? Most markets have too much small office inventory and nowhere-near-enough small and micro manufacturing space.

Based on what you're starting with for objectives and a building, how do you "match up" with what you want? Normally there is a discernible gap. Creative pricing, space, and services incentives come into play here to connect available resources with real opportunities.

Growing and managing a diverse incubator community of business establishments adds another layer of complexity to the operation. Building an occupancy plan starts by researching the history of industries and businesses that have already come and gone. Having done that, it is wise to learn why they came or left (or both). Economic legacy information, combined with current resource realities (physical, financial, human, geographical, etc.), can provide useful guidance at the start. You will form an incentive and support program accordingly.

It will take some period of actual operation to reveal the true current blend of opportunities and make the necessary adjustments. The process of attraction is a forever activity. It cannot be forced. Time, trial, and error are the most reliable keys to unlocking the secrets of **Entrepreneurial Gravity™** for your project. As we have said for years, "We learn by doing."

Smaller industrial rental spaces tend to be in short supply, but they can contribute to a broad spectrum of technology and innovation potential. We strongly favor targeting these sorts of enterprises. Office and commercial enterprises almost "take care of themselves" in the supply/demand arena. Industrial makers and artisans tend to need different infrastructure (docks, 3-phase electric service, sprinklers, etc.) Repurposing former factory buildings very often provides great mix options. There will be plenty of industrial space (if local DNA can use it). There's almost always some existing office space to rent and, in many cases, commercial options can be opportunistically created or added.

Incubator clients benefit from diversity and inclusivity in many ways. Different business sectors offer a variety of ideas to those in search of them. Businesses owned by people of different genders, cultures, ages, and abilities can inspire innovation as they reflect perspectives from the immense diversity of our world and the communities that house these places. The presence of wheelchair-bound entrepreneurs reminds everyone to be aware of greater accessibility in their processes, products, and services. Manufacturers and makers benefit from others who are makers or manufacturers of different components or different stages of their product production process. We learn more from folks who are different from us than those who are the same. Plus, we can build on that variety of expertise to expand our opportunities.

An example of this occurred in a mixed-use, multi-tenant, job-focused, industrial leaning incubator. There was a screen printer, a machine shop, and a metal coating business. Each of them would often encounter job opportunities that required a process they didn't provide. Drawn from conversations at networking events at the incubator, they formed a loose association. Anyone of them could be the entry point for new clientele.

A typical shared project looked like this: the machine shop would get an order for a product. The raw materials would come into the shared loading dock and go to the machine shop. The component would then go down the hall to the metal coating business which would provide plating or some other hardening coating. When this was complete, the component would go up to the third floor where the screen printer would provide labeling or calibration or other graphic elements. Finally, the finished product would be returned to the loading dock where it would be shipped back to the customer. This allowed each of the businesses to do more sales than they could have done on their own at better margins. If the product had to come in once and then ship out two more times to achieve the needed finishing, the bidder may not have been competitive on price or time or both. Because of the different activities housed under the same roof, the customer neither knew nor cared that multiple businesses were involved. This trio of local independent businesses was able to grow and prosper from their ability and proximity to cooperate with others.

Networking events

Networking events are a core element of many business incubator programs and are vital to mining the many treasures of a mixed-use (or any) business incubator. At one of our job-focused, mixed-use incubators, the "Coffee and Cookies" event would see crowds that included business owners, employees, makers, artists, salespeople, technology workers, and more. People from all walks of life and different stages of life and culture and education had these regular opportunities to meet and explore their interests with others while waiting in line for their drink and sweet treat. Because they were all from the incubator, they knew they had a common connection in the building as well as in their entrepreneurial efforts and struggles.

Working partnerships, like the one described above, find their genesis in conversations at such events.

To maximize participation across any incubator's population, it is vital to try different times (morning, lunch, and after work), venues, goodies, and event programs. If you try enough "stuff," you can learn what creates the most value for your unique collection of business operators. We often find the most effective solution to include some variety that aligns with a particular group's diversity. For example, at the BIC, we usually did social networking events (coffee or bagels or whatever) in the morning and educational panels or talks after work.

While our story is focused on the incubator program, building, and the businesses they aim to serve, it should not be left unsaid that the host community benefits in several ways from the same diversity that makes the incubator experience more effective and more valuable. The community gains jobs from the employment priority of the incubator and gains financial strength from the businesses that bring in new money, and all of that circulates, supports, and helps grow new commercial and service businesses in a virtuous spiral up. In addition to the direct financial and creative value derived by the business owners, employees, and business program from inclusive diversity and mixed-use, the incubator and its host market benefit from enhanced energy and resiliency (operatively & financially). The entrepreneurs plant the seeds, the business incubator is the fertile environment, and the jobs, spending, taxes paid, and quality of life that grow out of this effort are the fruits of that investment.

Entrepreneurs, small businesses, incubator programs, and their host communities all are improved in positive ways by blending a mix of people, plans, and possibilities into a community of opportunity. There are both business development program and financial advantages and complications to planning, organizing, and successfully operating a homogeneous business incubator mission serving a heterogeneous collection of entrepreneurial adventures. When a project truly seeks to help people prosper in the unpredictable chaos of the "real world," an appropriate practice period in a mixed-use business incubator can be valuable in contributing to their survival and success.

"A lot of different flowers make a bouquet."

—Islamic Proverb

LESSON #3 IS THAT WE STRIVE FOR INCLUSIVITY, DIVERSITY & MIXED-USE.

CHAPTER 3 REVIEW

- Diversity enhances the function and longevity of BIs by maximizing the business and employment potential in a community.

- Mixed-use means a blend of industrial, commercial, office, and other business activities, spreading the financial risk over a broader base of business sectors, enterprise life cycle stages, financial strengths, and seasonal variations.

- Anchor tenants can be mixed with local businesses to provide financial strength, stability, and community impact.

- Homogenous incubators are risky because of economic, political, and technological pressures that could slow or end an industry.

- Networking events allow businesses of all shapes and sizes in the BI to benefit from each other.

Chapter 4 — Be Locally Owned & Operated

There's a saying in real estate that the three most important things for a property's success are location, location, and location. For a job-focused business incubator, or any local business center, this is true as well but for different reasons. Where you are in the world, in your regional market, and within your host community certainly matters. When focusing on job creation, the unique leadership, resources, and community participation in that place will determine its level of success. Decisions about how to strategically manage these sorts of elements affect what businesses will come to you and how you can (or will) help them. Nobody will care more about or be better able to demonstrate a willingness to work for your hometown, and its businesses' survival or progress, than the people who live there.

> *"If you don't know where you're going, any road will get you there."*

It all starts with someone's "bright idea" to start a business incubator. Defining what you want to accomplish with your business development center, and what you're willing to risk and commit to achieving it, may be the most critical decisions you make. Is your priority creating jobs, revitalizing the building, or something else? Are you coming from a place of desperation or optimism? Establishing your objective vision, and what you're going to measure to define that "win," establishes the "North Star" that will guide your journey to a successful project. Everything else in the process will flow from there. Simply put, when you know where you're going it's easier to get there.

For us the process often goes like this:

- Who's the project developer ("check writer")?
- What is the vision of ideal objectives? Often, they are jobs, financial sustainability, eliminating blight, or some combination of these. This establishes **The Strategic Project Mission™**.
- Prioritize that list and get down to the top three or four objectives.
- Define **The Objective Vision™** (for example "100 jobs and cash flow breakeven by year 4").
- With the clarity of that objective vision, we then sketch out the plan and evaluate the pros and cons of the building while identifying the strengths and weaknesses of the community.
- Compare those to the opportunities and challenges of the location, the economy, and the universe of realities affecting the situation.
- This is a significant "Go or No Go" moment. If it looks like there's a good chance to succeed, move forward. If it doesn't feel doable, it is better to walk away or change focus and explore again.

It should go without saying (but I will say it) that the measurable objective needs to be appropriate for the **realities of the place and time** you are working with. Projects in smaller markets or involving narrow sector targets (such as "only fintech software" or "robots for outer space") can suffer from inadequate deal flow and require eternal subsidies to survive. The broader "mixed-use" focus, with a preference for highly desired enterprises, is a more practical path.

It should be noted that once your local **Strategic Project Mission™** is defined, **The Objective Vision™** needs to identify your wins in measurable terms. This may include the number of jobs, property occupancy levels, or a deadline to achieve cash flow breakeven. Whatever the appropriate objectives may be for your project, they need to be made quantifiable to support future performance progress.

It matters who decides where you want to go. It is vital to long-term success that this individual or entity possesses a deep knowledge of and commitment to the project community. Their capacity to stay involved through the critical startup-to-stabilization years is paramount. Many people can be involved in the thinking and strategizing phases, but, in the end, whoever is accepting financial responsibility for the effort has to decide what return they expect on their investment. Is it jobs? Is it the renovation of a blighted building? Is it the attraction of new technology or something else? How much "outside" money will be needed or accepted? To effectively get started, one of the very first decisions needs to be "Who's going to write the check." Whoever is ultimately paying for the enterprise is the project developer, and that project developer — the check writer — defines the objective vision and what a measurable "win" will be.

The initiating force for a business incubator will, most often, be a local individual, a company, or an institution of some sort. This is a significant point for many reasons. Economic development is a "forever" and, ultimately, local process. If the community doesn't care enough to commit and lead (or at least, to not be an obstacle), the chances for success are severely diminished — perhaps non-existent. The source of that initial push often becomes the leader or project developer. When it's a private individual, often there are still others involved in the decision-making. In any case — individual, corporate, or institutional — it is important to collect input from all the appropriate people to prioritize and objectively guide the project along its way. Once started, hiring, buying, and communicating progress locally need to become and remain a priority. Few things generate support for a center and its startups like everyone in town (or someone they know) being involved or "touched" by the project.

These can be difficult but wonderfully fulfilling projects. They will take time, energy, and the involvement of the entire community either directly or indirectly (most often, some combination of the two) to be successful over the long term. For this reason, it is important to gather local input and participation. In projects developed by governments or NGOs [non-government organizations], public participation during the planning phase is common. Given a private or corporate project developer, in addition to market data, it is wise to find ways to collect the thoughts of local people. In the "old days," we would make a point of chatting with the gas station attendant, our server at a diner, and other "folks on the street." EDOs and chambers of commerce have a bias toward the positive. Too often the most vocal people are negative, while the "silent majority" almost always supports local job creation endeavors. For reasons like these, we have found it useful to hear some "unvarnished" opinions whenever possible.

Walking around and casually talking to people still yields valuable perspective. Today, local diners still offer good wisdom. Other potential sources include local hardware or home improvement stores, barbers/hairdressers, wine/spirits stores, and coffee shops.

It is worth mentioning that perspective can affect purpose and objective setting. As decision-making drifts away from a local challenge, such as to the state or federal level, the sense of urgency and customization of a solution diminishes almost exponentially per degree of removal.

Projects arise from a universe of situations. Some are hopeful (like attracting a new level of technology to the local ecosystem), and some are frightening (like battling 20% local unemployment). Both perspectives (optimistic and desperate) can, and sometimes need to, cause objectives to skew toward higher performance targets in shorter achievement times. It is wise to be mindful of your starting state and strive to identify the most likely "real world" possibilities. Hometown input is particularly valuable in such a case.

Next, consider physical placement as it significantly impacts facility sizing and how you need to organize your incubator program and building to be financially sustainable. There are pros and cons to every site. Strive to clearly identify and utilize the uniquely good. Be honest and beware of the bad. Your mission and the objectives and resources you're able and willing to commit locally affect the answers to what these are and how they can be maximized or mitigated.

When your primary objectives are the building and the margin, your objective vision is likely to include occupancy, cash flow, and return on investment. If you are primarily about the jobs, your objective vision is much more likely to include things like business starts, jobs, occupancy, and events with a nod to cash flow or net operating income (NOI).

Many times, people think they're about the building, but they're really about the jobs. Even when they know they're about the jobs, there's usually an affection for the building and its historic place in their hometown. Project developers may start from being about the building and then find that they "lean" towards the margin priority, as opposed to the job priority. There is a constant need to be clear about what business activity can honestly be attracted, supported, and helped to prosper in <u>that</u> place in <u>that</u> building at <u>that</u> time. Wrapped around and in and through all of that is the need to pay for the improvements, the investments, and the ongoing operations that achieve the vision of a job-creating, nurturing Business Center. The chances of successfully operating these sorts of projects will rely on maintaining your local connection and realistic vision because it is a multidimensional activity that ebbs and flows throughout its lifecycle.

For economic development groups, this should be a simpler decision-making process. Their primary measurable objective is often jobs or business starts and attractions. Still, depending on their funding situation, even EDOs can be pulled to turn their eye to how far to lean on margin to fund and achieve the mission. This attention impact can be exacerbated when the EDO folks are not native to the market, nor are they intending to stay there for a lifetime. Scarce dollars will tend to gravitate to the biggest project or candidate for the best ribbon cutting. This is another situation where "hometown" money and leadership may exercise better discipline to "keep hitting singles" instead of only chasing "home runs."

In many of our projects, we're working with an industrial building and we're pursuing manufacturing or industrial jobs. When our primary focus is jobs, we pay attention to a broad spectrum of businesses and their sorts of needs in the building and the services to be provided. In cases where we focus on manufacturing, this leads us to look for more particular things like loading docks, heavy floor loads, heavy power and sprinklers, and, if it's a multi-story building, freight elevators.

When we are more interested in physically and financially saving the building, our focus might change to location, subdivisionability, and what sorts of businesses can start, grow, and prosper there. Location and parking also become very important with commercial projects.

When settling on your objectives, please remember that **reality matters**. This is especially true within your particular **Entrepreneurial Gravity™** field. If your primary objective is jobs and you don't have a building, please look for one that supports a mix of business uses that are consistent with the local DNA When you start with a building, please target companies that might, actually, be able and interested in locating and operating there. For instance, former schools are notoriously bad for manufacturing but can transform well into office, commercial, and, if applicable, residential uses.

We have guided the revitalization of several large buildings and have seen how these can be organized to be self-supporting with their own staff, their programs, and their equipment when designed for their unique community and developer. The greater number of rentable square feet in a larger property allows the program costs to be spread out and more affordably supported. In smaller buildings or smaller communities, more thought needs to be given to the program that is provided by the center or, instead, partnered or outsourced to regional resources like SCORE, universities, or industry trade and networking groups to achieve ongoing financial independence. To reiterate, local decisions, resources, and depth of commitment are keys to getting this right.

In making these hometown decisions, it's helpful to have someone experienced in these sorts of endeavors to guide you through this process of exploring what your priorities are and what is possible in the reality of the place and the time you're seeking to perform. When you're an economic development group, partnership, or small city, village, or town, a group process is more advantageous as it provides multiple perspectives. Having someone with "hands-on" knowledge lead you through it can make it noticeably more efficient for the group to achieve consensus on **The Objective Vision™**. The quality of the process to determine how you define a win is vitally important because it will drive the majority of your subsequent development and operating strategies.

This startup exercise of documenting where you want to go is part of a process that may include a loop or two. When you look at your initial list of objectives and compare them with the realities of the DNA of your place, it may become clear that adjustments are needed to achieve your performance objectives of jobs or cash flow or whatever. Sometimes this gap is large enough to cause you to circle back to reconsider your objectives. This is a valuable step for multiple reasons, not the least of which is that, at this point, some projects can see clearly that their best path is to not start. Being realistic about that "Go" or "No Go" decision is an important benchmark in the decision about whether or not to deliver a job-creating business incubator.

In addition to having the motivation of a community-driven mission, there is a practical requirement to also have a reasonably secure

49

commitment to the time and resources expected to be needed to accomplish it. When the commitment to time, which could be as much as six years to initially breakeven, and/or financial investment, which varies by project, is not firm and foreseeable for the needed future, it is a far less painful path to avoid starting it at all. Searching for better alternatives that can and will be fully realized for that situation will be the wiser path.

Even when the decision is made, in the light of these initial findings, to proceed toward a start, there can be another "Go or "No Go" decision point once **The Strategic Blueprint™** is clarified and quantified. It is less common, but if the environment, the needed investments, or resources have changed enough, it can dictate a delay, restructure, or walk-away situation. These sorts of commitments and decisions are best made by those, locally, who will be needed to stand up and deliver on them.

Having decided to "GO", it is **always** important to operate as locally as possible. The incubator's team wants to be full of community faces. You can train folks on how to manage an incubator, but you can't train them to be a local citizen. As many contractors and professionals as possible should be local. In buildings with legacy systems (elevators, boilers, and such), the specialty contractor may need to come from elsewhere but can sometimes train a local service person. In any event, the more people from the community you can get involved with, the better it is. The project gets to positively impact lots of people and, in the process, creates many, many salespeople. Folks tend to encourage and try to help efforts that they are touched by, directly or indirectly. The more voices spreading your story increases the opportunity for that information to reach someone you want it to reach.

A particularly unique expression of local personality is the collection of decisions about how much, if at all, to subsidize an incubator's startup and/or operation. Many business development centers require some sort of one-time grant or gift for their acquisition and startup phase. However, in some grants, gifts, or subsidies, there can be requirements embedded in the transaction that add cost, deflect the focus, or otherwise surrender some autonomy to the donor. These are appropriate requests from the funder and are generally considered as a cost of the endeavor. This is typically the case in "one and done" capital gifts. When the situation changes to operating subsidies from governments, foundations, or NGOs, it can become more complicated. Bypassing the potential deflection of focus scenarios, there is a foundational issue in choosing to pursue or accept some or any subsidies. It is the rare operating subsidy that lasts forever. At the same time, our experience indicates there will be three to six years of operating losses before the BI becomes self-sufficient. Given that, does your BI business plan depend on finding evergreen sources of assistance (such as grants, cost credits, or multiyear donations) for the center's lifetime or strategizing a path to "wean" off at an appointed time? All of the centers we managed (mostly EDO but several for-profits) chose to limit and, as soon as possible, eliminate operating subsidies.

Differences in operating decisions are reflected on both sides of the income statement. Pricing decisions about above-, below-, or at-market pricing say as much about financial needs as the developer's fiscal approach. Incentive pricing, utility reimbursements, and tenant-make-ready investments are more examples of uniquely discreet local decisions. How to organize the project entity (non-profit, for-profit, etc.) varies by situation because of risk profiles, funding stacks, and mission/margin balance. Even beyond that, we have worked with EDO-developed projects that strove to achieve financial stability while offering below-market occupancy costs, invoking their tax-free status (among other tools). Other local EDOs were organized as non-profit and tax-free but chose to pay full real property taxes because they felt that helping maintain the tax base was as important as their job development mission. Every one of these decisions had implications that then needed to be addressed in leasing, networking, building operations, and other project realities. Local willingness and ability to trade money, time, and the risks taken to capture businesses, jobs, and local prosperity takes an almost infinite variety of shapes, sizes, and decisions. Your hometown's approach will shape what is possible in that place. It is important to tell the truth about what may be possible at your location, in building and executing these long-term job-creating projects.

During the three to six years from startup to stabilization, market forces will be clarified in action and will often change along the way. This operational reality requires the ongoing measurement of project performance against your objective vision. This will guide you to make adjustments needed to protect the mission's progress in a timely and strategically sustainable manner that continues to align with your community's ever-evolving needs.

Just like any other journey, defining your destination, creating a map to guide your travel, and constantly tracking your progress while you adjust for unexpected obstacles and detours, is your best strategy for success. Making these decisions and commitments locally is vital to the health, survival, and positive impact of your incubator throughout its existence.

LESSON #4 - BE LOCALLY OWNED & OPERATED

CHAPTER 4 REVIEW

- Decisions about how to strategically manage local leadership, resources, and community participation will determine the BI's level of success.

- Defining ideal objectives like jobs, financial sustainability, eliminating blight, or some combination of these determined the **Strategic Project Mission™.**

- **The Objective Vision™** quantifies your wins in measurable terms like number of jobs, property occupancy levels, or a deadline to achieve cash flow breakeven.

- Be clear about whether you are really about the building or really about the jobs as you determine what business activity can honestly be attracted, supported, and helped to prosper in that place in that building at that time.

- Be honest — honest about the DNA of your place, honest about the funding opportunities, honest about the level of community support, and honest about your true objectives. Without these elements in place, searching for a better place is the better choice.

- It can take three to six years from startup to stabilization and as many as six years to reach breakeven. So, a commitment of time and resources will be necessary from startup through to profitability.

- **The Strategic Blueprint™** dictates the environment, the needed investments, and resources needed to launch.

Chapter 5 — Find Ways to Help Them

The first step in helping entrepreneurs start up and grow (after you've created an incubator program and environment that can truly contribute to their success) is to find them at all. If you can't find them and you can't talk to them, you can't help them. How do you "draw them out of hiding?'

Independent local startups are notoriously difficult to find. There's no list of "people thinking about starting a business," so you have to make it very easy for them to find you because it's unlikely you're going to find them.

One of the important ways that an incubator helps in your town is by being a visible symbol of opportunity for people wanting to start and grow a business. Here is where the physical presence of the building is vital. It is a visible symbol to everybody in your ecosystem that there's a place to go to get help. It can serve as the nexus and center of service, support, and resources from regional partners to help people in your market area to start and succeed on their entrepreneurial journey.

A business development center can serve as a magnet for new businesses by having a credible reputation for encouragement and nurturing. The best marketing is a successful track record of helping others. The services and events at the center, along with the successes of the businesses housed there, can get the attention of early-stage businesses and people exploring the idea of a startup. It may take some time but what you hope for is to be known as the place to start and grow a business in that region.

Outreach efforts can cast a bigger net and help more people connect with your program. Selectively opening up appropriate training and networking events at the incubator to the public are examples of this practice. We have also had success finding new folks by targeting strategic populations with special pricing to coincide with focused periods like Global Entrepreneurship Week, Women Owned Business Month, and National Crafting Month. This is just a sample of other ways to communicate to the market that this is a place that will support and nurture a variety of businesses to improve their chances to succeed and prosper.

One of the reasons we are so focused on self-sustaining business incubator facilities is that the most powerful attractor of the next business is a solid track record of success by other enterprises from that center. That sort of credibility is only earned over time. Financially independent incubator facilities are important - that they exist at all - because they model good business practices in their daily operations for clients and tenants.

Once you have a contact interaction with the small business owner, it's vital to learn how your project can create value for each unique situation. We find that asking lots of questions, in person, yields a variety of values. Besides the obvious things (What's your product/service? How will you make money? Why should we believe you can do this? Etc.) You can learn a lot from how they answer. When they can't or won't respond to key questions, it can be an indication that they may not be ready to get started or be "coachable" enough to benefit from the program Along the way, you start to build a relationship that will be needed for both of you to be happy with the journey you're about to go on together. It should be noted here that this step is critical to saving a lot of lost time, money, and heartache from situations that lack what's needed to, at least, have a "fighting chance." Every prospect isn't ready or is a good fit for your center. One of the most valuable roles you can play is to tell them the truth and direct them to "go back to the drawing board" or pursue another path entirely. Sometimes, they should just get a job.

For those folks that fit your target criteria, there should be space and services that reduce some risk, enhance their capacities, and support their ongoing business evolution. Everybody needs something, but it's seldom everything. If it is "everything," it may be worth reconsidering if your prospect is ready. Some business owners may need to work more on their plans and funding. This unique recipe of assistance that you design to attract people to your center and enhance the survival and success of their diverse entrepreneurial endeavors of all sorts is known as the business incubator's PROGRAM and it comprises three broad categories: space, services, and wisdom.

SPACE

Our incubator efforts have always been focused on jobs and recycled buildings. In the beginning, we pursued almost exclusively manufacturing, and we reasoned that such businesses would need space to house the people, processes, and products. Although economies have evolved so that, now, we strongly prefer mixed-use business centers, it still holds true that most job-producing businesses need industrial, office, or commercial building space. For this reason, physical space, properly managed, can become a tool, as well as an operating advantage, for the entrepreneur.

With manufacturing, makers, and artisans, space is very important to their capacity to create. People who are working out of their garages or their basements can only grow to a certain level before their further progress is stymied. The limitations that block their expansion go beyond simple square foot measurements. Depending on the product, at a very early level, makers and manufacturers can need things like bigger utility infrastructure (electric, gas, water, sewer, and internet), truck-level loading docks, sprinklers, and workspaces with higher ceilings. The ability to utilize these sorts of advantages provides leverage to their unique abilities to do more <u>faster</u> and more efficiently than they would have otherwise.

As soon as small makers and other little businesses try to "move up" to commercial space, they are confronted with the risk of multi-year lease obligations for inflexible areas that tend to be larger than they need. It is not unusual for a commercial landlord to require a five-year lease commitment.

The incubators we operate in recycled industrial and commercial buildings strive to provide as much space flexibility as possible. It starts with a selection of smaller units, such as 300, 600, 900, or 1,200 square feet. It's more than these folks have at home, but it's smaller than what the commercial market likes to provide. Lease terms for startups can vary from month to month for up to three years, depending on the situation. In addition to offering smaller units, there is often an option for startups in one of our facilities to "flex up" on a short-term basis to capture some unexpected opportunity and then "flex down" afterward to their original footprint.

For us, "flexing" indicates a temporary increase in space to help people try things out-usually to take advantage of a buying opportunity or extra space for a big order. The tenant uses & pays for the space on a monthly basis and then returns it when done. The rent then drops back to its lower base. Sometimes, after "flexing up" the tenant keeps the extra space. In that event, it gets added to their agreement and is no longer a "flex" situation.

In the beginning, very few founders can accurately predict the size and timing of their space needs. Allowing maximum, practical flexibility for the first three years allows everyone to try things out and learn what the reality may be. When they "graduate" from the incubator, they've learned how to be a tenant and are much better prepared to make good decisions in the open market.

In addition to providing better physical space, these sorts of business centers can contribute financial advantages to the small business operators by tailoring leases and rent structure to each particular situation. Considering the job creation potential, the quality of their plans, and other aspects of each particular opportunity, a center can often calculate and provide a unique rent program. There might be a graduated rent program that's lower at the beginning when they're getting started and cash flow is always a challenge.

Another method may be to build in strategically timed free rent months (even when rent is free, clients should pay whatever variable costs they create, such as utilities or services consumed). Another financial advantage to entrepreneurs of locating in a business incubator in a recycled building can be faster and less expensive access to utilities. Often, utilities like power, gas, water, and sewer are already in place and paid for by the incubator. Even though well-managed centers track and get reimbursed for utility usage, the new business can be up and running the same day without paying costly utility deposits or waiting for credit approval.

While some shared services cost money, shared facilities can deliver precious savings to the business owner. Many incubators and local business centers offer a variety of shareable conference and training rooms. Industrial centers may provide shared staging and loading areas. These sorts of amenities allow fledgling enterprises to operate from a smaller footprint, which reduces their occupancy cost. Once again, every dollar they don't spend is a dollar they don't have to earn, or, even better, is a dollar of profit.

These are just examples of the many ways risk is reduced for the entrepreneur by the incubator. The incubator creates value by serving as an insulator or "shock absorber" of operating costs for its clients. Instances like this, where operating costs of the startup can be avoided, delayed, or "smoothed out" amount to what we call "backdoor financing." Every dollar the startup doesn't spend on necessary costs like rent and utilities is money that they can invest in the operation of their business. It's also money they don't have to borrow from a bank or equity that they might give up to an investor.

When focusing on businesses that will create jobs in your hometown, the space itself can be an attraction while the creative strategic management of that space can multiply the magnetic pull and opportunity for your targeted entrepreneurs. It is particularly gratifying when the innovative revival of an obsolete structure is nurturing the birth and growth of small businesses at the same time it is being resurrected itself.

SERVICES

Direct business services are an important component of the program value of an incubator. In the early stages, few people accurately predict their staffing and equipment needs. Even if they do, the operational demands of the leaps to each new level of performance can be financially jarring. Incubator management can mitigate this challenge by identifying common needs for their targeted sectors and then arranging appropriate shared services. This can be a critically important resource to small business establishments because it allows them to only use what they need until they confirm that they can fully utilize and afford that staff position or piece of equipment.

Some of the sharing we've seen included stuff like high-performance copiers/printers, forklifts, delivery trucks, and additive printing equipment. Labor can be very difficult to predict, so some centers share staff with clients to perform bookkeeping, tech support, manufacturing, delivery, and other business services. As the businesses and the incubator grow and evolve, the menu of services and shared stuff inevitably changes to serve the current reality.

Shared equipment is a great way to attract and help your priority job-creating businesses. For makers and artisans, expensive items like kilns, laser cutters, or high-end 3D printers can provide capacity and a chance to explore new technology before investing in it. Textile startups might benefit from commercial sewing machines and floating pattern tables. Food makers need the use of a shared commercial kitchen in the early parts of their journey. Wet labs, particularly small ones, can be very difficult for science innovators to access. Most businesses today covet big and fast bandwidth, but data centers and software development also covet redundant connections and generators. As you "zero in" on your primary job creators, it becomes clear where the gaps and "pain points" are that your program might strive to solve.

Some community and university incubators can assemble useful collections of pro bono professional services for certain startup situations. The most common categories appear to be legal and accounting among a broad diversity of assistance depending on target sectors, geography, and incubator developer connections.

WISDOM

Shared knowledge and experience may be the most precious component of any business incubator's program of assistance. My dad used to tell clients that we've made most of the mistakes already and can save them the trouble if they'll listen to us. Time and money are almost always at a premium. When we can help someone avoid a costly misstep, particularly during their fragile startup phase, it is especially valuable.

This distribution of "knowledge resources" gets done in a variety of ways. The incubator manager is often the coordinator and first dispenser of wisdom. Regular monthly interviews, brown bag "lunch & learns," and "just dropping in" to talk are all valid ways to hear what's going on with a business owner and have an opportunity to share useful advice. Arranging peer panels on interesting topics and offering onsite training are more structured delivery systems. Networking events with peers and resource providers can be remarkably rewarding. Properly done, these sorts of "coffee & cookie" or "wine & work" events can accelerate creative collisions at the same time they connect to the greater ecosystem that the center resides in.

Many startups are not aware of the layers of support in a region. Fortunately, many areas have a variety of entrepreneurial and economic development assistance. Because the incubator's team is focused on jobs, they should be "tech agnostic" and be able to guide the business founder across the regional resource "silos" to the most appropriate programs for each unique situation. Introducing them to resources like SBDC, SCORE, university programs, entrepreneurial mentors, and venture funders that are present in your ecosystem increases the incubatees' capacity and broadens their opportunities.

We feel that one of our best roles in the startup process is as a "gap filler." We strive to coordinate and cooperate with all the resources in the ecosystem but, sometimes, there are pieces of support that are needed but missing from your place. The ability of an incubator or local business center to respond to that resource gap by identifying and securing it from the ecosystem or providing it somehow in-house is a significant value-creating feature.

Please be reminded that nothing happens immediately. All of this takes time. The unique character of your community and your project developer shape the project and the program that revitalizes the building and contributes to your economy. You start with your best sense of what's needed in the community at the beginning, but it takes time to develop. Over the years, you'll learn what the market needs and what the market wants; the gaps you need to fill to create value become clearer to you and to the market.

It takes time to build a reputation as a reliable positive nurturing environment for business. In the beginning, it often takes a year or two for the market to understand how to use the incubator. During that same time, the incubator staff and developer should be continuously reviewing their activity to "zero in" on the most important value creators to business establishments in their market.

Our decades of activity lead us to believe that entrepreneurs benefit from a mixed-use incubator experience. The opportunity to see and interact with a variety of different business sectors and operations is an innovation instigator and accelerator. While the center's program strives to do this in a structured and orderly manner, the layout of the physical space and the supportive management of a mixed community of businesses delivers an endlessly fertile ground for serendipitous interactions to spark new progress.

It has been our experience that more resources exist that are focused on high-growth, scalable business concepts than on the universe of independent local businesses. With this in mind and recognizing that we believe every business is important because every job is important, we prefer to build our programs to focus on and serve the greater number of independent small businesses, recognizing that the occasional high-growth venture will show up from time to time.

We are guided by our principle of "cooperative self-reliance" to structure programs to take advantage of partners already active in the ecosystem for the 5% high-growth venture opportunities while we build our programs to focus on the other 95% of independent businesses. We strongly believe that a good incubator or business development program is open, accepting, and helpful to everyone. We accomplish that by building our facility program for the local folks and then partnering for the resources needed by that smaller number of high-growth opportunities that inevitably appear in any market. It is always our goal to create value for everyone who seeks to access the program.

It has become very clear to us, over many decades of helping thousands of businesses fill millions of square feet of buildings and create countless jobs in the markets we serve, that we are not smart enough or clairvoyant enough to know for certain which businesses will break out and become a gazelle or unicorn. There is hope in every business startup. Even though we don't always see the possibilities at the same level as the client or take as much comfort in the business plan as they do, if they have enough of some things and are willing to invest and risk their time and energy, we strive to support that effort as much as practically possible.

At the Harvester Center in Batavia, over the years, businesses of all shapes and sizes learned to come to the industrial center where they were met with open arms. We worked to welcome them with creatively structured situations that might help them to start and grow. Some of the examples of actions that attracted and encouraged businesses include helping them:

Start Faster
- A gentleman showed up in a pickup truck towing a trailer with a cement mixer and molds for decorative outdoor objects. He explained his plan and his eagerness to get started. An appropriate space was identified that already contained the needed utilities (all of which were already "on" as part of that center's operating principles). The lease was signed, and he was active in business and pouring cement molds that same day.

- A small Canadian business had a significant opportunity suddenly arise that would require them to set up a manufacturing plant and start producing their product within a week. Suitable space was located, facility staff worked with local contractors to install equipment, and calls were made to coordinate the needed numbers to be hired. The deadlines were met, production got underway and, in less than a year, the firm graduated and bought a building, which they later expanded to meet growing demand.

Regroup Faster

- When a local shirtmaker's building was destroyed by fire, 7,600 SF was found in the local incubator which allowed them to resume production in less than two weeks. Over time, the shirt company's output grew, and a retail component was added. They grew to occupy over 200,000 SF of buildings in a 100-year-old structure with multiple shifts and over 150 jobs.

Scale Faster

- A packaging materials business was started by a small group of partners in 4,000 SF of a much larger industrial incubator. Their business flourished and grew to over 100,000 SF with 90 jobs. They graduated and built a 90,000 SF building in the same county.

Operate Cheaper

- Two local men started a utility and safety product distribution company in the incubator in 1,400 SF of office and, later, added another 1,000 SF of storage. As their enterprise evolved and they realized how much more time they were away from (instead of in) the office, they were able to give up that space (and cost) by utilizing the shared conference room for their monthly team sessions.

- As a result of one of our women business owner networking events during "Woman Biz Owner Month," a local jewelry maker moved into the incubator. She took advantage of a special offer for attending the educational networking event and received three months of free rent. Her business has benefited and grown as a result of having this affordable shop to concentrate on her craft.

It is exactly because we can't see the future, and we don't know how markets or technology will change, that it is so important for us to help everyone we can who has an appropriate business plan. Some plans may be on a napkin, some are in a 50-slide PowerPoint presentation, and some are just in the entrepreneur's head. We try to create programs that provide value and increase the survival and success rate of as many businesses as possible. While every project has its unique personality, there are often commonalities (accounting, pricing, employment practices, and the like) that are already being addressed somewhere else within the ecosystem. The opportunity to create innovative ways to use whatever inventory of resources may exist is one of the keys to success and survival for a business incubator or local business center in its effort to contribute to community prosperity.

Your unique combination of building space, a program of support, and management of culture is what defines the possibilities for your budding business owners. It is also what differentiates you from a commercial real estate investment. Guided by your objective vision and ecosystem realities, you have the opportunity to craft an environment that creates value and promotes progress for the potential entrepreneurs within your gravitational pull. Because every job is needed, help as many as you can.

LESSON #5 IS YOU MUST FIND WAYS TO HELP THEM

CHAPTER 5 REVIEW

- Independent local startups are difficult to find. Make it easy for them to find you by being a visible symbol of opportunity in the local place. The physical building serves as a visible calling card.

- The BI must become the center of service, support, and resources in your market area, known in the community as the place to go to start and succeed on their entrepreneurial journey.

- The best marketing strategy includes a successful track record of businesses in the program, events at the center for incubatees and non-incubatees, and services offered to help others.

- Choose incubatees who are "ready" for the program based on a well-defined screening program that looks at their business as well as the owner's level of commitment and coachability.

- The BI's program consists of space, services, and wisdom it offers.

- BIs help businesses start faster (when they are eager to get moving on their idea), regroup faster (after a loss), scale faster (in response to sudden growth), and operate cheaper.

Chapter 6 — Strive For Financial Independence

Job creation is a never-ending endeavor.

Locally owned, operated, and funded business incubators or a local business center can be the foundation and the engine that energizes that entrepreneurial ecosystem. This works best when the center is grounded in the community and has the resources to move as fast or slowly as its market needs. Subsidized programs seem to eventually run out of donor support and need to close, morph into something, or get absorbed into some sponsoring institution. When you can fund everything locally, you improve the odds of successfully serving local businesses for decades.

Long-lasting, impactful, job-creating incubators find a way to organize a building and program of assistance that serve their market and are sustainable for the long term. Maybe that's funded by a leprechaun's pot of gold! More likely, however, they have strategized to size it to their ecosystem and, usually through trial and error, settle into a careful balance of program/mission and funding/margin.

Funding everything from successful building operations is great whenever possible. We feel this works best with buildings that are 50,000 SF and larger. Some combination of property rents and service fees is often needed to "pay the way." How do you organize a business incubator so there's a productive job-creating program that's suited for and supported financially by the market within your **Entrepreneurial Gravity™**?

It is our experience that managing healthy flows of funding into what we call The Three Buckets of Money is the key to having the margin to achieve your mission.

The Three Buckets Strategy™

The Three Buckets Strategy™ is an integral component concept of The Strategic Building Solution™

Business incubators, like any value-creating business, need to get started, find a way to be profitable, and continually improve to address changing customer needs. Each bucket needs to be filled, in some prescribed order, so that it can fill the next. The metaphorical buckets serve those stages as follows:

The Startup Bucket - for acquiring the facility, renovating as needed, and funding the operating losses until operational breakeven is achieved and then fills…

The Operating Bucket - to generate positive cash flow to build a cash reserve and, in turn, fills…

The Improvement Bucket - collects surplus operating money to fund program and facility upgrades to meet the evolving needs of the entrepreneurial community it serves.

All of the buckets are important. While each project's details will vary, the interrelationship and general tendencies are likely to be consistent.

The Startup Bucket

It is said in commercial real estate investment circles that "you make your money when you buy." Similarly, the composition of funds and structure that go into "buying" the start of an incubator project significantly impact its future ability to survive and thrive over the long term. The Startup Bucket is used to pay for initial acquisition and improvements to open the doors of your Center and fund its operating losses until stabilized operating breakeven status is securely achieved. At that point, having bridged the facility to operating profitability, it will have provided the resources to start to fill the operating Bucket that will carry the progress forward.

Things that go in the Startup Bucket include gifts, in-kind services, donations, grants, equity cash from investors and/or developers, equity labor from the developer, and various sorts of debt (please be warned that, while a loan ADDS to Startup Bucket cash, the repayment of that debt will SUBTRACT from Operating Bucket cash for years).

When you are assembling this bucket, it is important to be aware that all funding is not created equal. Each sponsor and investor has an agenda that exerts pressure on your operation. Developer equity is generally in complete alignment with the project's mission. Each additional source is likely to focus on a KPI [key performance indicator] or rate of return that can dilute or deflect your direction. It is wise, to the extent it's possible, to limit capital sources to those most in alignment (or least likely to conflict) with the project's strategic objectives.

What should come out of the Startup Bucket are the pre-acquisition costs (design, assessments, studies, etc.), the acquisition costs (purchase price, closing costs, environmental remediation, etc.), and any other investments that are needed to get started (roofs, utility metering equipment, initial subdivision renovations, etc.).

In managing the various buckets, you are wise to try to keep the Startup Bucket as low as possible and avoid funders with unrealistic expectations. While this is ideal, it is seldom achievable. The Startup Bucket is a strategic balancing act. Keeping it low helps you get to the Operating Bucket sooner, but if you don't invest enough to get the right facility and make the right improvements to function as needed, the startup "savings" may get chewed up paying for operating losses longer until you get to break even.

Strategies for managing the Startup Bucket are as different as the countless unique situations that call for them. With that said, reducing operating costs as quickly as possible is always helpful. A technique that we've used more than once in large industrial buildings is investing in dry sprinkler systems that can reduce the area and cost of heating major vacant spaces. In one case, we were able to convert a $40,000 sprinkler change into a $60,000 per year heating cost saving. Another fast return, upfront renovation is installing utility measuring equipment that can allow "passing through" usage costs as tenant reimbursements to reduce the owner's expense burden and improve the net operating margin to the developer.

The Startup Bucket is difficult to fill. It also happens to be the phase where grants and public assistance may be more appropriate because, generally speaking, the donor's restrictions can often be limited to the renovation event and may not complicate future operating flexibility. Having the building donated or having the funds to buy or improve the building donated is positive but tends to be a "one-and-done" deal. Sometimes, with local foundations or other donors, the same philanthropic organizations are present and willing to contribute to future improvements, which is really helpful.

Buying and building property is not the only way to acquire a business incubator facility. Downsizing industries have been known to donate their surplus factory to the effort to replace the jobs being lost by their leaving. It can be mutually beneficial as they may reduce the carrying cost of a shuttered building. In at least one situation, the departing corporation "sweetened the deal" and mitigated some of the project developer's risk by leasing space back to help cover the new owner's operating cost and accelerate their progress to the Operating Bucket.

One of the more interesting creative startup deals we were involved with included tenant participation. We managed an industrial incubator facility for many years before the property was sold. The new owner chose to self-manage the incubator. After a few years of deferred maintenance and non-incubator operations, the project fell into financial distress. There was an opportunity for a different owner to buy the center and bring the Mancuso Group back as incubator managers, but there was an insurmountable gap in the funding needed. One of the growing tenants we had placed in the project years earlier learned about this situation and offered to "fill the gap" by expanding its footprint and prepaying three years' worth of rent! This unexpected investment in everyone's future led to a successful transition. As a footnote to that event, that tenant went on to graduate from the center, buy a vacant factory, and become one of the largest industrial employers in that rural county.

The Start-up Bucket and the Improvement Bucket are the most appropriate and generally speaking, the easiest buckets to attract grant funding. In the U. S., the majority of grants tend to favor capital investments, such as buying or improving properties. I'm told that, in Europe, there are more operating subsidies than in the U. S., which helps their Operating Buckets. On the other hand, in developing countries, every bucket is a challenge.

Wherever and whenever you're trying to capitalize a business incubator, creativity, flexibility, and a strategic assessment of any and all possible sources of money are the keys to filling the first bucket with "The Right Stuff."

The Operating Bucket

The Operating Bucket is the lifeblood of every incubator and center. This is defined as the positive operating cash flow that exceeds capital reserve targets and/or any debt service coverage. A critical goal is to find a way to achieve profitability from just the property and the program to protect the life, survivability, and sustainability of the operation. Some incubators utilize a different core money generator such as a benevolent corporation with extra space or an operating business that seeks to "give back" to the community. The Operating Bucket needs to generate an appropriate rate of return on invested capital with sufficient surplus to self-fund focused property and program enhancements. The success of the Operating Bucket is what fills the Improvement Bucket to fuel the cycle of improvement review-revise-improve that's important to the long-term survival of any endeavor by always producing current value for clients and investors.

Things that go in the Operating Bucket include rents, expense reimbursements, program fees, service fees, events, and investment returns. The stuff that comes out of the Operating Bucket can be utilities, property taxes, insurance, staff payroll, program costs, facility operations, and marketing.

One of our primary strategies for Operating Bucket success is to utilize the property as a funding tool and maximize the building's occupancy at the right rents via strategic creativity. Some revenue-accelerating examples we have employed look like this:

- **<u>Tactical Reduced Rent</u>** - occupancy is the key to income. The sooner your facility achieves its targeted stabilized occupancy (commonly considered by financial institutions, to be 85% to

90%, even though it can be cash flow "stable" at as little as 30%, depending on the situation), the better your results will be. Timed and targeted "rent sales" are a way to generate buzz about the center's program and accelerate client decision-making to move in. It is important, in these sorts of incentives, to still require the client to pay for utilities and other applicable expenses generated by their presence.

Occupied space with no rent that covers its costs is better than high-priced vacant space. The incentive will later "burn off" and the center will then enjoy the full relationship that, otherwise, might have been missed. In addition to advancing operating income, the startup has benefitted from lower occupancy costs and experienced the center's commitment to startup success. Typical, *crazy* creative rents are focused on getting job-generating business targets to take action <u>now</u>. Variations have included three months free for WBE and two months for artisans who lease by a certain date. If it's just a market deal (for whatever reason), it just wants to be enough discount to seal the deal.

- **<u>Cluster Businesses Visibly At The Front</u>** - when starting a project from scratch, to overcome "Pioneer Tenant Reluctance" (no one wants to be first into an empty building), the initial clients are, as much as possible, positioned at the front of the building. This communicates activity and positive progress to encourage subsequent businesses to locate and grow there. At the Batavia Industrial Center, the first occupant in a million-square-foot factory was a 1,200 SF sign maker that was positioned on the street level so that people would see that "the lights are on at the BIC."

- <u>Events</u> - many business incubators serve as the "Crossroads of the Entrepreneurial Ecosystem." Networking and training events at the center are important components of its program of support. While these sorts of events are free to tenants, inviting others to attend for a fee can be a useful tool for new and small market incubators. In addition to helping clients improve their business and generating money for the Operating Bucket, these events contribute to Word Of Mouth [WOM] marketing for the center and its program.

Somewhere, now lost in the mists of time, a wise man said, "Every dollar you don't spend is a dollar you don't have to make." From before you begin all the way until after you end, managing expenses is an ever-present task. This becomes a particular challenge in an incubator or business center because it costs money to operate facilities and deliver assistance to startups and small businesses.

Every situation is unique. Building size and age, program complexity, and market resources are just a few of the many variables that confront you when starting or operating one of these mixed-use, multitenant, mission-driven projects. A few of the more impactful strategies that we have used include:

- Only Operate What You Need - Lights, heat, elevators, and manned security are examples of operating costs in large or partially vacant centers that can be cut back to save money until they are needed and can generate appropriate revenue. As the program prospered and businesses moved into the vacant areas, tenant-paid heating systems were installed to protect the savings. The same principle applies whenever there are multiple units of something such as elevators, cranes, or buildings on an incubator campus.

- Match Staff To Activity and Income - Strategically align payroll costs with facility size, income status, and expectations. Often, the beginning may be part-time staff (or shared staff, if there are satellites nearby). As the project can, add staff as needed and afforded. During such a ramp-up in a team, it can be very helpful to partner with regional ecosystem resources for value-creating programming. In smaller projects, it may be wise to stay with the part-time team + ecosystem resource model.

- <u>Operating Expense Reimbursements</u> - Every enterprise has a unique direct cost profile. By having clients reimburse the incubator for some, or all, of their variable direct costs, the business is incentivized to manage the expense while the center, and other clients, avoid the additional burden. By using this pricing model to control costs, the incubator maintains greater flexibility in pricing and its ability to provide rental incentives for other startups.

At certain stages of an incubator center's development, having an appropriate anchor tenant can provide some needed cash flow. Public- or education-owned properties can, sometimes, reduce or eliminate property taxes to save money. Each project's situation craves creativity in addressing its unique challenges and opportunities to generate its own needed money.

Another job of the Operating Bucket is to fund a cash reserve of, ideally, six months of operating expenses to protect the project during the inevitable "ups and downs" during its lifetime. In tandem with, or after, fulfilling the Operating Reserve target, it is important to build some amount of Capital Reserve to fund expensive replacements of infrastructure components like HVAC elevators and sprinkler systems. It is especially important to have such a fund when dealing with "legacy systems" in older buildings.

The Improvement Bucket

This is the bucket responsible for enhancing the property and the program to meet the ever-evolving needs of clients. Every business incubator, its clients, and its market area are constantly changing in multiple ways. As this occurs, to stay relevant and deliver value-creating space and services, the center needs to be able to respond "at the speed of business" (in other words, "quickly"). Rapid, market-driven decisions happen best when you already have the money. Delays and divergent agendas are, too often, a cost of using "other people's money," such as public grants or incentives. As much as possible, debt should be avoided because, among other issues, it burdens and reduces the net operating cash flow needed to feed this fund. For these reasons, this bucket wants to be built into your center's overall plan.

Operating Bucket surpluses are the core money supply for this effort. Other contributions to the Improvement Bucket can come from stuff like developer equity, grants, and prepaid rent. Earned and donated money are scarce resources that can be creatively leveraged and extended in different ways. One method is taking advantage of donated and pro bono services, such as marketing or internet support. Another effective technique is allowing a tenant to perform and pay for its own direct improvement. Similarly, when investing in an upgrade that serves only a portion of your client community, a shared reimbursement assessment can be created for that specific cluster of enterprises. Installing a redundant power supply or a backup generator for certain tech firms are examples of such situations where the operator organizes and upfronts the money to implement the focus group's desired improvement. At an urban mixed-use project with multiple tenants that we were managing, there was a discussion that led to the initiation of a seasonal, evening security service to escort folks to their cars after dark. The service was organized and implemented by the operator. Its users were limited to participants that, in return, fully reimbursed the operator for this program enhancement.

The variety of potential downstream changes to a program and property is as variable as the kaleidoscope of people, places, and purposes striving to succeed around our world. In the revitalization of an empty or larger facility for service as a business incubator, the subdivisions for new startups, the creation of or expansion to networks of hallways, upgrades to utility infrastructure, and the other building reconfiguration costs of converting, growing, and expanding in an existing building are common examples. As your project and program mature, the needs of particular clients can call for HVAC changes, windows, and other things you discover you need to do along the way such as improving handicapped accessibility or energy conservation. Cluster evolutions may lead to wet labs, shared commercial kitchens, or maker space investments to fully embrace and encourage the diverse universe of hometown opportunities that exist.

A revolving loan fund, additional staff for programs, buying time with targeted online experts for training, and anything that nurtures and supports a client's startup or small emerging business, that is learned and added along the way, is an improvement to the business incubator and/or local business center that can increase the value creation of this center if your bucket is "healthy."

It is crucial to the long-term success that the facility finds a way to dedicate a portion of its income to keep the Improvement Bucket full enough to contribute to positive progress adjustments promptly.

LESSON #6 IS YOU MUST STRIVE FOR FINANCIAL INDEPENDENCE

CHAPTER 6 REVIEW

- As you can see, there are different stages in the life and service of a business incubator. Each stage needs money. Many incubation programs rely on a steady stream of subsidies from the government, education, foundations, and other philanthropic institutions for their capital and operating financial needs.

- Generally speaking, public funding in the United States has favored capital investments while, it is our understanding that, in some other countries, government or philanthropic funding of business incubator operating expenses is more to be expected. Wherever you are, and whatever your economic development objectives may be, tell the truth about your realities and structure the lifecycle funding of your strategic blueprint accordingly.

- Ideally, you would fund from successful building operations like rents and service fees. But this is not always possible, especially in the beginning.

- Generate healthy flows of funding from the Three Buckets of Money: Startup Bucket, Operating Bucket, and Improvement Bucket.

Chapter 7 — Recycled Buildings Can Save Time & Money

You might ask "Why any building at all?" People certainly talk about, and think they operate, "incubators without walls." But to me, that's just a program of assistance. Call it what it truly is.

In contrast, a business incubator is tangible, existing as a visible, physical space. There is credibility and a message of commitment to the mission that goes with that occupiable space. Physical space is an important part of the support program for growing job-creating businesses. On top of that is the reality that the building is an integral component of how to pay for the program and achieve the financial independence needed to survive and serve your mission.

With that said, why do we feel so strongly about using existing buildings?

"Because they're there!"

There's something compelling about a large, empty building that cries out for attention. Sometimes they're beautiful or full of history or just too big to ignore. But, in every case, I'm always struck by the investment of time, money, and materials that was justified by the prior activity and the opportunity that still, somehow, lingers within to be captured and benefit the next, yet-to-be-determined, user.

Properly reimagined and revived, these structures feel like a gift from the past to unlock a better future. The key is solving the mystery of identifying and implementing their new value-creating proposition.

My friend and fellow adaptive reuse aficionado, Steve Asbury, says:

> *"Every building has a unique personality. We need to understand who they are so we can take advantage of their gifts."*

I believe their very existence is often the first gift when it inspires someone to take action that eventually benefits a community. Even during the process of their revitalization, buildings can offer physical, financial, and strategic advantages in the quest to sustainably create local jobs.

When confronted with a community or regional-level challenge of any sort, but especially economic, there is a lot of inertia, driven by fear and uncertainty that must be overcome to take any measurable steps forward. The physical presence of a facility that can house an industrial, commercial, and office business incubator or local business center can provide a visible rallying point of hope for a timely counterattack to current economic obstacles.

Job-focused, mixed-use centers in old structures, almost by definition, will demand strategic creativity in their funding and operation. Fortunately, our experience demonstrates that some or all of the following advantages of existing buildings contribute to their startup, stabilization success, and survival:

- **Faster start** — It's already there! Existing infrastructure can include larger electric service, truck docks, sprinklers in place, and immediately shareable areas (a big advantage to small &

artisanal manufacturers that struggle to find small shop space with "big building" features).

- **Faster money** — You can begin the process of generating revenue immediately from rentable sections (BIC started with 1,200 SF, Harrison Place with seasonal vehicle storage, and the 800,000 SF West End Business Center with a 300 SF office).

- **Cheaper Capital & Operating Potential**— It can cost 5x+ more to build new Starting from the ground up is "all or nothing" as opposed to incrementally easing into something that's already there while you're figuring things out.

- **Cash Flow Accelerator** — You can spread out startup investment costs by starting with a "digestible" section and rehabbing as you grow (market guided & cash flow managed). With a new building, there is a huge upfront investment for someone. In addition, lower cost + faster revenue = shorter climb to breakeven.

- **Location** — Buildings are often in walkable places that offer services and options for a more diverse entrepreneurial population.

- **Flexibility** — Old buildings tend to have smaller floor plates and column spacing that encourage making the smaller units that are needed in every market. Use what you need or what you can and grow into the rest. The ability to "flex up" using vacant existing space is a definite advantage. (Flexibility is a "two-edged sword" in old buildings as you learn to work with and/or around the existing structure and legacy infrastructure systems.)

- **Character** — older facilities are already woven into the fabric of the community and its people and history. Some may be officially historic. The familiarity of the site and its connection to different generations offers a level of comfort as well as inspiration from the prior success that is responsible for its presence in the first place.

- **Green** — It's already there! Save the environmental cost of new construction plus avoid demolition and landfill impacts.

The sprawling 50 to 70-year-old Massey plant was an unlikely "beacon of salvation" in 1959. The success in refilling such a cavernous empty shell demonstrated possibilities inherent in other idled factories. From that first small sign maker, additional tenants of varying sizes were attracted to locate and grow. For some, walls were built. Others, with rapid growth plans, occupied larger spaces and were billed according to the progress of a chalk line that indicated their space use. When the chalk line stopped moving, the wall got built. There was always room for that unexpected something or someone with an idea. Rent income (meager as it was) started and was able to grow incrementally at the speed and cost of the market. Using this same method, we were subsequently asked to lead industrial multi-tenant revivals in buildings from 80,000 SF to 800,000 SF, which then inspired the productive reimagining of other sorts of obsolete, empty, or underutilized structures such as former schools, department stores, and military bases.

Notable reuse examples developed by others include the Fulton-Carroll Center (350,000 SF in a former South Chicago factory), Della Clark's The Enterprise Center (36,000 SF in the original American Bandstand studio in Philadelphia), and the 2,000,000 SF Brooklyn Navy Yard in New York City. Intencity, in France, led by Alexandre Meyer, operates multiple incubators, such as their 4,000 SF Paris Center and the Clichy site with 20,000 SF.

Our system can be seen in action with a project we worked on in a small city (population 21,000). A 500,000 SF campus of 2- and 3-story industrial buildings just one block off Main Street that the city had taken for back taxes was losing big money, operating with only a few tenants. Due to this, and its blighted condition, the city requested a $2 million grant for demolition from the state and evicted the remaining tenants. When that request was not filled, we were able to show a way, for far less than the $2 million, to bootstrap the campus to profitability for the city by strategically focusing on one building at a time and instituting a business incubator focus.

The fruits of our labor began with a 600 SF overhead door repair business. It took a year or two to build market credibility, but the nurturing culture of management and the center's operations continued to attract small businesses. Some of these grew bigger until the rentable space was 80% occupied, there were over 250 jobs created or moved to the city, and the site was generating positive cash flow from operations. Eventually, it began to repay the developer's startup investment in improvements and funded operating losses accumulated during the four-year climb to cash flow breakeven.

In this instance, because the building was already there, we were able to start immediately. Revenue began to grow very quickly because we could take "all comers" (especially the underserved micro-enterprises) and still stay flexible enough to take all normal-size businesses. The location also helped by allowing leasing to commercial, office, and service uses, after initially being limited to industrial uses by the nature of the building, while establishing market credibility. We were able to accelerate cash flow progress by using part-time staff and minimal investments until more expensive improvements became affordable.

Every situation is different, but you get the idea.

On the other hand, if you wanted to build a job-creating, mixed-use incubator or business center from scratch, pre-design decisions must be made without the "real world" guidance of the market. Ideally, the starting mission objectives provide enough of a starting point. Given a job-focused, mixed-use vision, some blend of mixed-uses needs to be targeted for some portion of the project. Do you build out 25% or 50% of the building? Of the portion you renovate to start, should it be 50% industrial and 50% commercial or 70% industrial and 30% office? In any scenario, what suite sizes do you preconstruct? It can be done, it just requires more thought, tolerance for risk, and money.

We are familiar with a small city (population 13,000) that decided to build a brand-new, high-tech incubator building to elevate and diversify its workforce and economy. Technology experts were brought in, and an attractive 20,000 SF state-of-the-art tech facility (offices, wet and dry labs, and small storage) was designed and built for more than $2 million. From the beginning, the facility struggled financially. A small research tenant's production of a liquid nutritional product "took off" and consumed the vacant, unfinished space. The lab suites were never fully utilized and, eventually, were dismantled in favor of more usable offices and shop space. The high-end HVAC was another challenge from Day One because it was designed for a theoretical operation that never occurred. After years of operating losses, an additional round of public grants and loan forgiveness was secured to be able to afford significant renovations to reflect a more local market-focused facility.

Even if you design a perfect mix at the outset (whose crystal ball is that accurate?), by the time it gets built 5 years later (it often takes 3 years to raise money, before spending 2 more years to construct), the market will very likely shift requiring a different mix than you planned. By that time, a lot of money has been spent, the time has passed, no businesses have been helped, and the center's facility will be "wrong" for the current conditions. Changes would be needed at the outset anyway. Since the existing building is already "wrong" at the start, you can spend those waiting years incrementally improving the old building to respond to known market requirements. Because there is a need to renovate, either way, existing tends to prove to be cheaper and faster.

While we're on the subject, as a cautionary tale, you can also overthink and over-prebuild existing space. To help a local industry expand, a small city ended up owning a 200,000 SF, early 20th-century factory. In pursuit of jobs, they decided to create a business incubator. They secured a sizable federal grant and other assistance to build out a predetermined assortment of industrial and office suites of varying sizes. They creatively housed a city department in a portion of the factory as the anchor tenant. After some initial leasing success, the project fell on hard times. When we were engaged to improve the situation, we quickly identified significant operational saving strategies to slow the "bleeding." Given the size of the market, it was clear that many of the prebuilt suites were simply too large. The combination of the saving and leasing changes, plus weaving in a previously absent program of business assistance and networking efforts, enabled the project to move from a 6-digit operating loss to cash-flow breakeven and the ability to start self-funding some improvements.

The moral of these, and similar stories, is to not overly pre-design and build anything. A strength of existing buildings is that you can start leasing from a corner and incrementally build out the space as you're guided by the local demand. We have found the most success by "renovating as you go." Find a rentable room or two for showing and leasing at the start. If there simply is no "market-appropriate" place to start, it may become necessary to construct a model space to either rent and then duplicate or utilize as a pattern to guide future improvements as businesses arrive. Over time, the needed inventory develops. The key here is to maintain the patience and discipline to grow with your market.

When you build a new building, there's a huge cost and it's all at the beginning when you have the least revenue. It's "All or Nothing." Given new construction costs, project developers tend to "only build what we need." This normally ensures that there will be little or no extra space for any runaway (or, even, moderate) success stories. If the outside market does not have "second-step" space for businesses that "graduate" from the center, they may be forced to leave the community. We have been reminded many times that, for lots of reasons, we are not smart enough to reliably see into the future to predict "winners and losers." This is one of the lessons that leads us to strive for "overflow" or "success space" at each center. In its absence, it becomes extra important to identify other local options for those sudden or explosive growth situations.

The usual cost of "used buildings," relative to new construction, leaves room to acquire more square footage for the same or less cost. That extra space can come in handy when a:

- 4,000 SF startup packaging business in Batavia, NY grows to 100,000 SF with 90 jobs in three years (then builds a new building).
- 5,000 SF American. satellite boot sewing operation of a Canadian company expands to 180,000 SF, two shifts, and 240 jobs in three years.
- 1,200 SF woodworking enterprise morphs into a 15,000 SF artisanal glass maker and school in a small rural city.

Unexpected disasters can be ameliorated, and sudden opportunities captured by an incubator or Local Business Center with available space:

- When a fire displaced a 7,600 SF shirtmaker in a small town with a big incubator, they were able to quickly return to production because heated, dry industrial space with adequate electrical power was immediately available. Over time, business growth took them to over 200,000 SF and 300 jobs.

- A Canadian manufacturer secured a significant contract on short notice that required all production to be done in the United States. On three days' notice, an incubator provided 7,000 SF of generic industrial space and then "made magic happen" by using its resources and connections to interview and hire the needed staff, assist in unloading and activating the needed machinery, and find creative ways to "fill the gaps" in operations until the client could self-stabilize.

With an existing building, you can start small and rent a piece at a time. When needed, you may respond to unforeseen events to protect or capture jobs. The ability to tackle your project "bit by bit" or, when needed, "in a hurry" speeds up your revenue growth and helps manage your operating costs.

Many existing buildings are located in pedestrian-friendly areas. Old factories, abandoned department stores, churches, former schools, and other unused non-residential structures tend to be well-woven into the fabric of the place where they are. Downtown factories or former department stores can lend themselves to retail, service, artisanal making, technology, and other people-intensive activities. Repurposing these well-located but "oversized for the market" structures allows new generations of entrepreneurs to take advantage of this unique value handed down from the past. Their connection to the community they reside in and the lives of its people is an advantage that's difficult for greenfield, new construction in suburban sites to duplicate. In addition to reducing demand for driving, their reuse offers opportunities for a greater variety of uses and diversity of business owners.

For very small or micro businesses (particularly solo entrepreneurs), this combination of a diverse, dynamic, entrepreneurial community, with an environment that encourages moving about is attractive for the convenience, companionship, and increased creative collisions that become possible.

As an aside, the need to adjust to the existing legacy structure, as you try to implement a new value-creating use, is a constant and humbling reminder to pay attention to the realities of where you are, who you're working with, and what you're trying to accomplish.

Simply put, existing buildings can be bootstrapped in a way that new buildings cannot. Since many project developers or communities are seldom rich with financial resources, the ability to start small, bootstrap, and grow incrementally as your market guides you, is often the difference between survival and failure for such an undertaking.

If you have enough time, money, and commitment, I suppose almost anything can be made to work. In our experience — in the real world — existing is better as long as it's the right size with the right plan for its developer.

We'll talk more about all of this in the next chapter.

LESSON #7 IS RECYCLED BUILDINGS CAN SAVE TIME AND MONEY

CHAPTER 7 REVIEW

- Recycle existing buildings because they are there, to protect the environment, to save costs of new construction, and to adjust with market conditions and local needs. Besides, older buildings speak to the architectural and historic connection of the community they are in.

- Existing buildings offer many advantages new construction cannot, including faster startup, faster stabilization success, and better chances at survival.

- Existing buildings allow BIs to start small and rent a piece at a time.

Chapter 8 — Size Matters

Big enough to do the job and small enough to fit your mission's market. That's "the sweet spot." What does that look like? The answer is <u>always,</u> "It depends." The balance for each prospective incubator situation of program, building, and **Entrepreneurial Gravity™** is an infinite variety of variables for this formula:

The Business Incubator Recipe™

$$\left(\begin{array}{c} \text{Project} \\ \text{Sponsor} \end{array} + \begin{array}{c} \text{Job} \\ \text{Mission} \end{array} \right) \times \left(\begin{array}{c} \text{The Right} \\ \text{Building} \end{array} + \begin{array}{c} \text{Sustainable} \\ \text{Plan} \end{array} \right) = \begin{array}{c} \text{Job \& Business} \\ \text{Growth} \end{array} !$$

The Project Sponsor (or Developer) and Job Mission establish the objectives. The critical components then become the building and plan that creatively and practically reflect the realities of your market.

Depending on where you start for your project's mission, your sizing considerations include the following:

- More programs = more building or more volunteers/partners (maybe both)
- More building = more program + mix + anchors + *???* (depends on market size/velocity)
- More tenants = how small can you go? Small, micro, pop-up, shared shop, or office spaces

93

Our model has always worked to use the property to pay for the program. For that reason, we start with the building and work out from there, always keeping in mind the realities of that unique place.

We have worked to revitalize and fill industrial and commercial buildings from 9,000 SF to over 1,000,000 SF. These properties are in communities that range from a village of 2,000 people to MSAs (metropolitan statistical areas) with populations of more than 1 million. This is possible by strategically breaking a bigger space into smaller pieces for multiple businesses of various sizes and sorts, following the mission objectives of the project developer. Every situation is unique and offers "do and don't" ideas for others. All sizing is relative to the market, mission, and developer resources. For the sake of discussion, some general comments about size and sizing follow:

BIGGER BUILDINGS

We have come to think of 100,000 SF of industrial buildings as the starting point of "big." When it fits the situation, it's attractive because it provides enough rentable square footage to distribute the overhead program costs with minimal pricing distortion (in smaller buildings there can be upward pressure on rents to help pay for programs). The structure (ceiling heights, column spacing, utilities, etc.), layout (square, skinny, "jumble of buildings"), and condition all combine to make revitalization easier or harder. The ability to start somewhere and grow incrementally is one of the keys to survival and success. Larger facilities often offer more opportunities to do that. Another advantage at this size is that, depending on market velocity, incubatees can "graduate" from the program and avoid the disruption of an untimely relocation that forces them to move before they are ready. As long as there is still room for new startups, these stabilizing firms may transition to anchor tenants that can mentor and be a good example to incubatees while also bolstering the financial independence of the incubator.

94

SMALLER BUILDINGS

As building size goes down, demand for structure, creativity, and ecosystem partners goes up. With room for fewer startups, entry and graduation policies need to be focused on accepting and nurturing the most mission-appropriate clients as efficiently and effectively as possible. Three-year graduation limits are fine for some situations but can be highly disruptive to a small business that has "burned up" its three years of incubation and still isn't financially and operationally stable. Still, in sub-40,000 SF facilities that have high deal flow, it can become an issue.

With fewer rentable square feet, small properties struggle to fully cover their program overhead from real estate operations. This is a common scenario for considering above-market pricing for stabilized incubatees and anchor tenants (if any). Service and event fees, along with sponsorships and other forms of ongoing subsidies, become requirements. The pursuit of this sort of revenue needs to be innovative and honest in presenting what entrepreneurial progress hopes to be bought with donated funds. In smaller markets, linking multiple sites to share staff and other resources or connecting with a university or appropriate economic development service provider are other ways to manage margin while delivering on the mission.

BIG PLACES (population 50,000+)

Is it big and dense or "spread out?" In either event, larger populations, by virtue of their size, offer a more "target-rich environment." More people, in their uniquely variable way, will lead to more potential startups and business owners. It also means more diversity and chances for inclusivity in <u>every direction</u>— age, education, race, sex, financial capacity, experience, etc. There will be more competition for attention within the bigger city's higher volume of "noise." An incubator can offer buffering from the confusing noise and some clarity on paths to navigate the regional ecosystem. These communities can, often, support a greater number and variety of incubator programs. More people, depending on market DNA, offers a better "fighting chance" for effective specialty or limited focus programs.

Larger mixed-use facilities (100,000 SF+) benefit from and can deliver more diverse, innovative opportunities in these sorts of situations.

Within the community, the sites will want to, ideally, be walkable to services and food as well as accessible to all sorts of transport, including trucks and trains for programs that serve industrial tenants and makers.

SMALL PLACES (population below 50,000)

Lower population numbers trigger the need to be as mixed-use as possible to capture and benefit as many businesses as possible. The demand to be very strategic in planning and building your program becomes particularly salient because there will, very likely, be less deal flow. Program partners from the regional ecosystem become critical to both client impact and financial sustainability. Sizing will be wise to consider; pay attention to **Entrepreneurial Gravity™** in determining the market opportunity. A neighborhood or suburb hosting a project may, itself, be "small" but will function more like a larger place. The plan for occupancy mix, support programs, networking events, and other entrepreneurial encouragements should reflect these realities. Depending on the situation, some small places can "play bigger" than they are by executing a well-designed and connected regional vision even if their setting is rural.

Generally speaking, larger communities better support bigger incubator facilities. Still, we have multiple examples of smaller places where they also work well. One instance is a small city of 21,000 people (the combined city and town "metro" population is 42,000) that is home to a 500,000 SF incubator facility in an adaptively reused campus of two and three-level former factory buildings. With a mixed-use format, this project has flourished. Whenever you narrow the focus of your facility and your program, the market shrinks, and the project plan should reflect that. For this book, and driven by our experiences over the past decades, our starting perspective for sizing and programs relates to job-focused, mixed-use incubators.

Small facilities can work but require a little more planning. If they're independent, standalone centers, the cost of dedicated staff will exceed the ability of the building to absorb the market without exceeding local area rents, leaving no money for other operating expenses. One solution to this particular challenge is to deliver the program with a part-time site coordinator and volunteers. Working with volunteers and ecosystem partner connections can be the key to achieving financial sustainability. Another concept is to become a satellite for a larger network of incubators. Small facilities in big markets have more options because deal velocity and volume change their pricing opportunities. These are some examples of why location and size matter and that telling the truth about your situation and what resources are available is very important to design a project to achieve your strategic purpose.

Entrepreneurial Gravity™ is a big reason location matters. It is the recognition that the gravitational pull to a business owner of entrepreneurial assistance has limits. It generally appears in the form of 80% of your activity coming from within an 18- to 24-minute commute radius from your location. In rural areas, this may equate to a 20 to 30-mile circle, while, in an urban setting, it may only extend 3 to 5 miles, due to traffic or use of public transit.

Communities with incubators tend to be regional hubs of entrepreneurial activity. Some might invoke the age-old question of "what comes first, the chicken or the egg?" Does the regional hub grow out of the incubator, or does the success of the incubator reflect its location and magnetism within the region? My father used to say,"

We improve your opportunity for success because we've already made so many mistakes and seen so many things." Our experience, all other things being equal, is that the presence of an effective business incubator significantly contributes to making a place the center of an area's business development energy.

Another variable that affects sizing will be urban versus rural. In New York State, there's a big difference in demand and resources between New York City's 20 million people and the village of Arcade's 4,100. When planning an incubator, its job development program, building size, deal velocity, and volume for your market opportunity will vary significantly by community size, composition, and location. These are among the many considerations that should be addressed in planning and design. While it's true that bigger buildings provide more opportunity for business centers because the program and administrative costs can be spread over a broader foundation, this can become problematic in a small rural market. Big buildings can work anywhere if the conditions and plans are correct. This can be especially true, taking into account the sponsor's mission, financial resources, market dynamics, and other realities of the location, when that oversized property can become a regional economic development asset. A big building that is, as my brother Bill used to like to say, "centrally isolated" may cause difficulties in the strategic creation of a conventionally attractive program.

Just a few more thoughts on these important categories:

URBAN

The combination of population size and density can offer greater potential possibilities. When it's there, take advantage of the cornucopia of diversity to build a resiliently creative community of opportunity. A heavier mix of small to medium size spaces helps to serve the population (generally the commercial real estate market will take care of the larger enterprise needs). The expected availability of kaleidoscopically inclusive assortments of people and uses, carefully curated, can "amp up" the level of innovation by virtue of the broad spectrum of perspectives, processes, and possibilities, "jumbling together" in the cauldron of networking event energy.

Bus routes, rail, and other public transit can be attractive to entrepreneurs and workers. Walkability matters — from post-industrial districts to gentrified neighborhoods and everything in between. Parking is more of a "thing" in urban settings. Having parking on-site is best, but not always possible. Considerations will include whether any is provided. Is it paid or free? Reserved? Paved? And so on.

RURAL

According to USDA Economic Research Service's "Rural America at a Glance 2021 Edition, there are far more rural counties [1,976] than metro places [1,166]. However, the urban population [285 million or 86%] in the USA is greater than the total non-urban count of 46 million or 14%. Despite that fact (or, maybe, because of it), there may be a greater need for small business encouragement and support in those spread-out places due to their particular circumstances. Identifying resources available to capture the unique market opportunity of each small town or city is both harder and easier in these locations. The lack of market activity, population, and political "muscle" make it difficult to attract much financial or public assistance. At the same time, that very scarcity of resources allows you to, very quickly, assess what, if anything, is obtainable beyond the project developer's assets.

One talented adaptive reuse guide, Steve Asbury, invented and applied **The 40-75-15 Rule** to attempt to assess the level of opportunity outside major metropolitan areas (bigger places). His approach considered these three factors to "tip the scale" for or against a project's potential:

- Is it within **75** miles of a major metropolitan area?
- Is the project more than **40** miles from that major metropolitan area?
- Is it within **15** miles of an interstate highway?

He reasoned that this accounts for the path of predictable growth. In his example, a city in Southern Wisconsin that meets the 40-75-15 criteria will eventually become part of the Chicago Metropolitan area. He felt it would be beneficial to invest in a property before that growth happens. It is an interesting way, and one of many, to try to discern future fortunes.

It has served us well, in multiple instances, to start by clarifying the developer's top project objectives. In most cases, there is a leftover building that is too large or functionally obsolete for the small market location to absorb commercially. Depending on the resources and DNA available, given enough time and money, there is often a creative bootstrap pathway or other options to achieve a sustainable level of revitalization. If the capacity and commitment to time fall short of what is needed, it will be best to <u>not</u> start. What gets misunderstood, in many cases, is that these sorts of projects are best started small and grown incrementally to match market demand and avoid "outrunning" precious, scarce funding. Discipline and determination, tempered by honest, reality-informed creativity are the keys to reviving an old factory or commercial building into a progress-contributing business incubator or local business center.

It is a constant balancing act to find ways to deliver the project sponsor's mission within the practical realities of the size of the building, the market, and the resources available. These variables, and their endless evolutions, place a high priority on starting with a sustainable plan, relentlessly tracking its performance, and correcting course as needed. The process starts by clarifying the many parts and recognizing the challenges and opportunities inherent in each, as well as their diverse potential reactions to different combinations of each. Once there is a reasonable starting plan, "you learn by doing." Find a way to start and constantly monitor performance, make adjustments, and "fine-tune" your job machine for the place where it lives. Recognize that each property and project is unique in its potential, so it is important to honestly assess your particular obstacles and opportunities for whatever size you're dealing with.

LESSON #8 IS SIZE MATTERS

CHAPTER 8 REVIEW

- Sizing helps you provide more programs, more building, and more tenants.

- Use the property to help pay for the program.

- Urban programs offer special advantages due to larger communities, walkability, and public transit. Plus, there are likely to be more small and medium size buildings available as opposed to large factories or sprawling campuses.

- Rural places may have a greater need for BIs due to lack of market activity, population and political involvement.

- Consider the **40-75-15 Rule** to help assess the opportunity outside major metropolitan areas where the building is more than 40 miles away from the city but within 75 miles, and 15 miles or less away from an interstate highway.

- Start small and grow to keep pace with market demand and funding.

Conclusion — Plant a Tree - Start Now!

"The true meaning of life is to plant trees under whose shade you do not expect to sit."

—*Nelson Henderson*

Nothing changes until some action happens. Objects at rest tend to stay at rest. These physics are as true in the lab as they are in communities. People who lack jobs and hope, and empty buildings that continue to rot, are likely to continue their decay without someone taking a risk. Solid solutions to complex challenges take time to develop their roots and fully bloom. The sooner steps are taken, the faster progress can be available to those who need it. Since everything takes time, finding a way to start is the key to positive progress.

We have seen that business incubators and building revitalizations can be started quickly and developed incrementally in many cases. Every mixed-use, multi-tenant endeavor takes on a life of its own. This is why building a new business incubator facility is such a challenge and why I have encouraged the idea of starting small. Being able to start with a portion of an existing structure, facilitates "moving with the market" to avoid getting too far down the wrong path for your **Entrepreneurial Gravity™** field.

Whatever your motivation might be to fill a building with businesses (NGO, EDO, entrepreneur, old building lover, or whatever), find a way to start, stay alive, and prosper, however you define that, for a long time. One of our fundamental beliefs is that "We learn by doin'." The learning accelerates and tends to stay focused on "real world" issues as soon as you get underway.

Establishing **The Objective Vision™ [TOV]** for your project starts with clarifying your primary goal:

"IT'S ABOUT THE BUILDING"
- When you're a private for-profit, striving to fill an old building with businesses, banks, commercial lenders, seller financing, and equity are your most common pathways. When appropriate, historic tax credits may provide additional help. If there are local or regional incentives, that can be a plus. Most often, the deal's just going to have to "pencil out" in the commercial marketplace.

- Mission-driven LDCs, EDOs, and non-profits will have more options. The challenge can be determining what public or donor assistance complements your vision, rather than inflicting regulatory and reporting friction, burden, and/or cost. Offering to host a university incubator program may be a way to create an appropriate anchor tenant to get you started.

"IT'S ABOUT THE JOBS"
- For private, for-profit investors, the mission is admirable but, financially, the deal will almost always have to stand on its own. Helping a "right-sizing" company survive (in a sale with partial lease-back) or bringing in an "anchor tenant" can be helpful to demonstrate both your intentions and financial

responsibility. The best bet for extra help, if any, will most likely be from local or immediate regional ecosystem sources.

- LDC, EDOs, etc. do <u>much</u> better in this "lane." Most places will have a variety of assistance layers. Almost always some federal or state ED or CD program applies. Local, regional, and philanthropic funding sources vary widely by location and are always worth investigating because, generally speaking, they bring greater market awareness and less "regulatory baggage" (reporting, random quotas, extra process steps, etc.).

Unless you have unlimited funds (it happens, but <u>very</u> rarely), the capital component of the initial phase (startup to stabilization) of a job and business-focused endeavor can be complicated and creative. **The Opportunity Analysis™ [TOA]** gives you some idea of what possibilities may be available. Based on which version of **The Strategic Blueprint™ [TSB]** you choose to secure your best chance for long-term financial independence and success, different bubbles of techniques can be open to you for pre-stabilization financing.

Business incubators and business-focused, adaptive reuse deals are seldom commercially conventional transactions. More equity or, more importantly, less debt or other obligation-based money, becomes very valuable to "breathing life" into these sorts of projects. Creativity, at this point, is priceless and limited only by circumstances, tolerance for risk, and applicable laws. We have found it useful in this initial phase to keep these objectives in mind:

- **ARRANGE THE AMOUNT YOU NEED TO START TO BE AS SMALL AS POSSIBLE** - But it <u>must</u> get you <u>all</u> the way to stabilization. To repeat my father's sage advice, "Every dollar you don't spend, is a dollar you have to invest in your future." This is particularly apropos here. Work you do yourself, bartering, starting small, buying used until you can afford not to, etc. are all ways to make the "pile of money" you need to attract more achievable. This is a challenge with

105

government-funded deals that prefer everything to be done in advance. Such a path dramatically increases the amount of time and money needed; at the same time, it significantly increases risk (market and financial).

- **REDUCE CASH EQUITY WHENEVER POSSIBLE -** Whatever your total capital stack ends up being, strive to save as much of your precious cash as you can for the inevitable parade of unexpected events. For larger properties, there may be a chance to sell (ideally pre-sell) excess real estate to manage deal size. If dealing with a "right-sizing" industry, there may be ways to start with almost no money by leasing (or subleasing) incubator space only as needed until reaching a previously agreed threshold.

- **GENERATE CASH AS SOON AS POSSIBLE -** including, when possible, before you are even open. Holding fundraising events can often follow project announcements but precede heavy expenditures. Most of the time, this means getting the first tenant ASAP and driving occupancy growth. "Nobody goes where nobody is." This wisdom from the webinar "Top 10 Things To Do To Fill Your Big Old Building" declares a critical reality. The first tenant can be the most difficult because "everybody" wants to wait to see if and how this thing works. Having someone lined up in advance or aggressively incentivizing a target job creator or innovator that will be a positive reflection in the ecosystem are good ways to get going. Depending on your project's size or funding (or both), it is wise, in this opening stage, to stay flexible and very aware of incentivizing the pioneer cohort of businesses that get you to your desired stabilization level of occupancy and revenue.

In all of this getting started stuff, it's important not to lose sight of your mission/margin balance. Private building revitalizations are inherently heavier on margin, so their distraction danger is smaller. Job-focused business incubators need to get to positive operating cash flow (margin) to be strong and independent enough to help their targeted businesses (mission), so there's always a challenge to manage that balance carefully. Larger buildings have the "luxury" of taking in a little more "margin" on their way to "mission" because they have the room and can, once secure, replace the "non-mission" tenants with mission-focused incubatees from a position of strength.

Every project scenario is unique in time, space, and circumstances. Staying focused on what your objectives are, why you're tackling this endeavor, and the project's peculiar realities, while respectfully seeking win-win situations will provide plenty of opportunities for creative problem-solving. Here are the highly condensed highlights of a small sample of how it was done on some job-focused projects:

- **Condense activity to battle blight**

A large manufacturer moved out of a factory in a small city and relocated to a new facility. Private development efforts were not successful. Property appearance and condition deteriorated, and the city was forced to take property for significant unpaid taxes. The title was given to the local development corporation. The 500,000 SF, four-building campus was considered "too much to handle" and state grants were sought to demolish and clear the site for redevelopment. The grants were not approved, and the EDO sought solutions to deal with their increasingly blighted and expensive to-operate factory. Our assessment of the situation indicated an opportunity to revive some or all of the property as a job-focused business incubator. Because there were no funds at this time to invest, we proposed the strategy of concentrating all tenancy and investments in a single building to save money and maximize impact.

A focused management plan was created with pricing, terms, and services aimed at attracting small (1,000 SF to 9,000 SF) industrial and commercial businesses with jobs to the usable dry and heated existing rooms and rentable areas that already existed. As occupancy and revenues grew, all available cash was re-invested into interior improvements and creating more small suites to match market requests. The visibility of progress and "lights on" created confidence that led to more leasing and a state grant to further the proven good work being done. With more rents, tenants, and buildings in use, the onsite staff grew to 2 and then 3 full-time employees. By year 5, the project's operating margin was in the black. All four buildings were in use. The project reached cash-flow-positive and financially independent and remained so for more than a decade. At the time of this writing, there are hundreds of jobs at the campus distributed among the 60-plus (and growing) diverse community of industrial, commercial, and office entrepreneurs.

- **Bootstrap from catastrophic job loss**

The community's largest private employer closed causing the loss of thousands of jobs in a small city. The 1,000,000 SF assortment of interconnected 30 buildings ranged from 50 to 70 years old and sprawled across 60 acres. Instead of allowing the obsolete site to languish for years, in an effort to minimize the economic damage and speed the replacement of lost jobs, a local merchant family bought the property and set off in search of a large company. When it became evident that direction would not succeed, the plan pivoted to working with any businesses that might produce jobs. Not knowing how long it would take to stabilize the costly campus, the owners sought ways to survive until they could fill the building with enough businesses and jobs to be successful.

The property was far larger than the local market was ever likely to need, so any easily divisible buildings and land were sold to help fund carrying costs. Jobs were the highest priority but there was way too much space to fill quickly. Because the geographic location was conducive to it, short-term warehousing agreements filled the vast empty buildings which generated rent and service fees to help operate and improve the buildings. Shared trucks, employee leasing, and equity investments in job-creating industries were among the many efforts to self-fund the project to financial independence. It took five years until revenues covered operating costs and then the project went on to serve the ecosystem for decades. Over time, the warehouses were replaced by a variety of small manufacturers, artisans, and other enterprises. The incubator's staff grew from 4 to 22 until eventually settling at 6. The project has gone on to serve thousands of businesses that provide thousands of local and regional jobs within the incubator and its many graduates.

- **Race for Occupancy**

An office building in a transitioning neighborhood on the edge of a metro CBD fell on hard times. 80% of the five-story, 16,000 SF, stone building was vacant. The city tried to encourage the commercial revitalization of the area from its industrial past. Private individuals saw the possibility of filling a need for a small job-creating business incubator. They formed a partnership, bought the building at a deeply discounted price, and engaged a professional incubator specialist to implement their vision.

The building was already divided into offices, so that would be the most affordable place to start and allow for less expensive renovations as they moved forward. This, combined with the low price, preserved precious equity which would be needed to cover operating losses during the startup phase. It was reasoned, correctly, that there is always a large unmet need for small and micro spaces for startups at the bottom of the "demand pyramid." A shared reception area, administrative services, meeting rooms, and parking were devised. Faster internet, better copier/printing, and other equipment were acquired. Networking events, business counseling, and startup pricing with space flexibility were implemented to create value and reduce the risk for the entrepreneurs. Incentivized pricing targeted businesses that would employ more people. The recipe of entrepreneurial encouragement was well received. Within 18 months of opening, the facility achieved 90% occupancy (from its 20% starting point) and positive operating cash flow.

B. Thomas Mancuso

It is worth mentioning, again, that maximizing your welcoming reach to the most inclusively, diverse spectrum of mixed-use enterprises appropriate for your mission will benefit everyone: startups find a home, the incubator moves toward a healthy occupancy, and the community gets jobs. Stay as streamlined and simple as possible for you and your clients.

Most people will understand the near-term value of helping job-creating businesses start and grow in your town. What too many people, politicians, and policymakers miss is the cumulative effect of decades of community entrepreneurial assistance. In addition to the obvious graduates who move out of the incubator into leased, bought, or newly built buildings with their jobs and tax base contributions, startups spin off other startups and networked economic activity accelerates innovation. Some of it happens fast, others take longer, and still, other benefits accrue over time.

There can't be any shade today unless that tree got started a long time ago. Find your way and START NOW!

"The best time to plant a tree was 30 years ago.
The second-best time is now."

—Chinese Proverb

110

About the Author

B. Thomas Mancuso, SIOR

Tom Mancuso has lived his entire life in and around industrial, commercial, and incubator buildings. His experience in all facets of their existence is evident in his ability to understand the complex factors affecting their success. He has led the management of projects that range from filling a vacant 680,000 square foot rural factory building with multiple tenants to revitalizing an underperforming 16,000 square foot urban adaptive reuse project into a vital and profitable small business center.

Clients have come to expect strategic solutions focused on their objectives and based on research and analysis. His willingness to explore alternatives builds confidence in the ultimate direction taken.

The Society of Industrial and Office Realtors recognizes Tom as a Specialist in Industrial and Office Realty (SIOR) based on his production performance and ethics. He became a licensed real estate professional in 1974 and is a broker in the state of New York. Tom has authored articles and addressed international audiences on the productive reuse of old buildings and business incubators. He is a graduate of the Rochester Institute of Technology with a Bachelor of Science in Business Administration with a minor in Accounting.

If you received value from this book, please take a moment to leave a review on the site where you purchased it so others can find it. Thank you for your support.

www.ingramcontent.com/pod-product-compliance
Lightning Source LLC
Chambersburg PA
CBHW011845200326
41597CB00028B/4718